Replacing the Rapture

Effectively Win the Nations by Replacing the Rapture with the Great Commission

PONCE LEON

Edited by Freda Artichoker.

ISBN-13: 978-1977707048
ISBN-10: 1977707041

DEDICATION

This book is dedicated to our Lord Jesus, who redeemed us from our sin through His precious blood, and to the Saints, my fellow laborers, to whom I hope this book serves as a tool that will help hasten the harvest.

CONTENTS

THANK YOU FOR INVESTING IN THIS BOOK

I want to personally thank you for investing in this book. It is my passion and mission in life to see the nations of this earth come to Jesus. A big part of seeing this come to pass is helping the Church to understand and fully believe that it is God's plan to fulfill the Great Commission. I want them to understand that not only is it possible, but that it will happen. I want the church to be gripped with the truth that the Gates of Hell set up on every nation, shall not prevail against the Church. For we are victorious, we will overcome and we will, through the Holy Spirit, kick down every gate of hell, in every nation, and they will be discipled, thus fulfilling the Great Commission.

If this message burns in your heart as it does mine. I invite you to partner with me to get this message out to believers in every nation. Go to PonceLeon.tv and click partner.

Thank you very much, and God bless you!

Pastor Ponce Leon

ACKNOWLEDGMENTS

A Special thanks to Freda Artichoker for editing this book, and to the Saints of all eschatological persuasion, who may affirmed or challenged the understanding I have received as the result of my study of the Scriptures on this topic. Above all, thank you Holy Spirit, for you are our teacher and the illuminator of Holy Writ, and of the mysteries of God.

WRITERS' NOTES

As we examine the Scriptures that so many use to teach the rapture, we will be investigating the topic of the rapture in general. We are not trying to prove or disprove any rapture position i.e. the pre-tribulation rapture, mid-tribulation rapture or post-tribulation rapture. I will let the people who hold these positions argue amongst themselves.

Although, our primary focus is to investigate the validity of the rapture, it is almost impossible not to touch on the many other end time events which come up like the great tribulation, the millennial reign, the resurrection of the just and unjust, the judgment, the new heaven and earth etc.

Events outside of the topic of the rapture may be discussed at a minimum. I may comment on some other topic but will not be providing a detailed explanation, for my goal is to examine the Scriptural text that many say support the rapture itself.

In referencing the Olivet Discourse in Matthew 24 and other parallel passages, it is important to note that I believe the context refers to Christ's Judgement on Jerusalem in A.D. 70. I will however, reserve commentary for future books so that I may stay focused on the immediate subject at hand.

I refer to Matthew 24 and other parallel passages, not because I believe these comings are of the same context and nature of Christ's future bodily advent, but because I wish to glean principles associated with His coming(s) that are universal and consistent whether past or future.

The primary purpose of this book is to reveal what the Scriptures teach concerning the rapture and what God's purpose and plan is for us in the here and now.

INTRODUCTION

The teaching of the rapture dominates Christian television and radio when it comes to the topic of eschatology (end time study). This as a byproduct, has had tremendous influence on how the Church lives today. It directly affects our attitude and perspective on whether or not the Church wins in history by overcoming or ultimately fails by being overcome.

We have been conditioned not to challenge the status quo concerning prevailing end time thought like the rapture. The attitude seems to be just accept it with its subsequent consequences, good or bad, right or wrong. This prevailing attitude to just accept it, is fueled by the fact that the rapture is taught by some of the most famous preachers on television. They obviously cannot be wrong and we dare not question them.

Of course, as I say this, I'm being a little facetious. I have however, heard a television preacher say, that if you don't believe in a pre-tribulation rapture, even if you are a blood bought Child of God, you will be left behind to endure great tribulation and wrath... ouch... Really? For not believing in the pre-tribulation rapture? That's kind of harsh... I do hope he was not serious.

Some people say eschatology is not so important as to merit serious study and contemplation. I disagree with that. Eschatology is not a side point to the message of the Gospel; it is the ultimate consequence of the redemptive work of Christ. It is the ultimate end towards which Christ died and rose again to achieve.

Having an attitude which says eschatology does not matter, is like being on a vacation with a certain destination in mind and not knowing how to get there, nor having a road map that will guide you.

Having the wrong eschatology is like being on a vacation to California, USA while following a road map that leads you to Florida, USA.

Having the correct eschatology is like being on a vacation to Victorious Faith Center in Oklahoma, USA while following a road map that leads you directly to the correct destination of Victorious Faith Center in Oklahoma, USA.

The matter of eschatology is a very important subject. Again, it is not a side point to the Gospel, it is the ultimate desired outcome for which Christ died and rose again. Therefore, correct eschatology, is like a road map that reveals to you the desired outcome (destination), while leading you by God's strategically designed plan for getting you there.

So the question that we must ask, is the rapture a part of correct eschatology? Is the rapture a part of the road map for which God takes us to our destined outcome? This book sets out to answer this question.

In order to answer this question, we will examine some of the most established and cherished teachings of the modern prevailing end time preachers. We will find answers to the questions like who does this earth belong to, God or Satan? Who's left behind, the wicked or the righteous?

We will also examine Scriptures like 1 Corinthians 15 where we get the phrase "being changed in a blink of an eye" and 1 Thessalonians 4 to determine if the phrase being "caught up" is proof of the rapture or does it mean something completely different.

We will also look at the historic writings of the early Church fathers and the Early Church Creeds and Confessions to determine whether or not there is a historical record that will prove that the rapture teaching was embraced by the earliest Christians.

We will put to the test some of the strongest arguments which are proposed in order to support the rapture teaching. We will determine if the rapture is a part of the road map which guides us to the divine destination for which our Lord died and rose again to achieve, or, if instead, it is a misconception Christians have learned to accept, which has taken us on a detour and hence delaying our arrival at the divine destination.

PONCE LEON

CHAPTER 1

A TRAGIC RESULT

One great tragedy that has taken place in Christianity is the unbiblical end time teaching, which places the coming of the Kingdom of God in the future, after the return of Christ.

Modern day Christianity has traded the victorious dominion of the Kingdom of God for a defeatist and escapist eschatology, hence giving the control of the earth over to Satan and his cohorts.

In essence, the destiny of the Believers to rule and reign with Christ on the earth has been exchanged for Believers who sit in spiritual lawn chairs saying "well this earth is getting worse and there is nothing that we can do about it but wait for Jesus to rapture us out of here."

It will be seen throughout the pages of this writing, a Believer conceding defeat and sitting back as a spectator contradicts what the Bible specifically informs the Believer. Christ did not leave a weak defeated Church on the earth. He left a powerful, living organism called the Body of Christ, His Church, which is filled with the power of the Holy Spirit. Christ gave all dominion, power and authority to His Body.

We are to rule and reign. We are to establish the reign of His Kingdom through the fulfillment of the Great Commission. Our attitude should be "We won, we are wining and we shall win!"

Christ has already conquered all enemies and placed them underneath our feet (Eph. 1:19-23). It is our job to walk in truth and live victoriously on the earth because Christ has established His Kingdom on the earth and we are to operate in it.

In the Old Testament you will read prophecies concerning the coming of the Kingdom of God. This presents the Kingdom of God as a future promise.

In the Gospels (Matthew, Mark, Luke and John) John the Baptist and Jesus proclaimed the Kingdom of God was at hand. "At Hand" means it is at arm's reach. In other words, it is about to show up, it is almost here.

Romans 14:17 says that the Kingdom of God is in the Holy Ghost. Anywhere that the Holy Ghost goes, the Kingdom goes. The Holy Ghost was given to the Church on the day of Pentecost and the Kingdom that John the Baptist and Jesus said "was at hand and about to show up," did in fact show up on the day of Pentecost.

After the day of Pentecost account in Acts 2, nowhere in the Bible will one read that the Kingdom of God "will come" (as still in the future), they will instead read "you are in the Kingdom of God" as Paul wrote in Colossians 1:13 (meaning that the Kingdom of God is a present reality).

We must understand that God has placed us in His Kingdom (Col. 1:13) and placed His Kingdom in us (Luke 17:21) so we can release its operation, dominion and glory on the earth (Num. 14:21, Rev. 5:10, Rev. 11:15).

One of the major misconceptions to hinder our ability to function in the Kingdom of God is the rapture of the Church. We were taught that the earth will get worse and our only hope is for Jesus to come and rapture us out of here.

What a horrid picture. It is comparing the Church to a group of soldiers in a war, who are surrounded by the enemy and their only hope for survival is for helicopters to swoop in and rescue them before they are all destroyed. I do not see that in the Bible.

The Bible states God has placed all enemies and powers underneath our feet (Eph. 1:19-23).

The Bible states we are Kings and Priests and we will reign on the earth (Rev. 5:10).

The Bible states Christ is coming back to a Glorious Church not having spot or wrinkle (Eph. 5:25-27).

The Bible states when darkness covers the earth and gross darkness the people... when things are very bad and there's trial, tribulation and persecution, the Glory of the Lord will rise upon the Church and there will be a great end time harvest of souls into the Kingdom of God (Isa. 60:1-5).

The trial, tribulation and persecution are not the end, but rather sets the stage for a great revival. You see the darker it gets, the brighter the Light of Christ will shine!

This is the very same thing Jesus experienced. The Son of God was to be nailed to the cross and put to death. Satan thought he had won. Satan thought this was his hour of victory but what he didn't know was this was a part of God's plan, to strip him of his power and authority and put him under the feet of the Church.

In this same way the Bible tells us, in times of great darkness and persecution, God will do His greatest work through the Church. I believe there will be persecution, but the persecution will only set the stage for God to do something great.

The false rapture theory however, takes our attention from our job to rule and reign on the earth and make disciples of all nations. Our focus has been on escaping and instead of living in faith and victory we are living in fear and escapism.

When we do not understand our mandate to reign on the earth and make disciples of all nations, we unknowingly, turn the control and dominion of the world over to the ungodly. The ungodly sets the agenda, determines the culture and decides what's acceptable and unacceptable. They will no doubt call good evil and evil good (Isa. 5:20).

If the Bible teaches the rapture then we should embrace it. But if not, we should find out what the Bible teaches, and make it our goal to live by.

I submit to you, as you will learn through this book that the Bible does not teach the rapture but instead, it teaches the present day reign of the Saints and the growth of God's Kingdom through the fulfillment of the Great Commission.

God's Word promises this earth will be filled with the glory of the Lord as the waters cover the sea (Num. 14:21) and through His glorious Church this will happen (Isa. 60:1-6, Eph. 5:25-27) because we are not escaping through the rapture but fulfilling our purpose as the Glorious Body of Christ.

CHAPTER 2

WHO DOES THIS EARTH BELONG TO… GOD OR SATAN?

Before specifically discussing the validity of the rapture, there are two main teachings which give the rapture doctrine strength. Teaching number 1 is "this earth belongs to the devil" and teaching number 2 is "in the rapture the righteous will be taken and the wicked will be left behind."

If these teachings are true, then this gives substantial support to the rapture doctrine, but if they are not true, then it does major damage to the whole concept of the rapture.

This chapter will put the first teaching to the test by answering the question "who does the earth belong to… God or Satan?"

The next chapter will investigate the second teaching by answering the question "who will be taken or removed from the earth and who will be 'left behind' to inherit the earth?"

When one hears the phrase "Left Behind" automatically, images generated by the "Left Behind" books and movies of Christians disappearing from the earth come to mind. One place that the phrase "Left Behind" comes from is in Matthew 24. Part of the next chapter will examine Matthew 24 to determine if that is really what the Bible is teaching. Truth should be determined not by what our favorite preacher says, what you read in the books or watch in the movies, but by what the Bible states.

Now we will address the first question, who does this earth belong to, God or Satan?

When I was a child almost every preacher stated, this earth belonged to Satan. When I started my research on this subject, I could not find one verse that supported this theory. Shockingly, the Scriptures reveal the opposite. They teach the earth belongs to God.

The verse that many quote when trying to prove that this earth is the devils is in 2 Corinthians 4.

2 Corinthians 4:4 In whom the god of this world hath blinded the minds of them which believe not, lest the light of the glorious gospel of Christ, who is the image of God, should shine unto them.

Upon reading this, many will say something like "Satan is the god of this earth" or "The earth belongs to Satan" but these statements are far from true.

In this verse we read Satan is god of this "World" not the earth. The word "world" is :"kósmos" in Greek. This word more correctly would refer to sinful man and their system of doing things. It is saying that Satan is the god of sinful man and their way of living.

This word "world" is the same word used in John 3:16: God so loved the "world" that He gave His only Son and whosoever believes in Him should not perish but have everlasting life.

John 3:16 states God so loved the world, meaning sinful man, not the earth. God gave His Son to save sinful man from their sinful ways. Therefore, in 2 Corinthians 4:4 where it reads Satan is God of this "World" it is not talking about the earth, but rather, sinful man.

Satan blinds the hearts of those that believe not. Satan is the god of all unbelievers but when they receive salvation, Satan is dethroned and Jesus becomes their God.

Many people were taught to believe this earth belongs to Satan since the fall of Adam. The belief is God gave this earth to Adam and when he was deceived by Satan, the ownership of the earth was transferred to Satan.

After the fall of Adam, God's message to Moses will eradicate this belief that Adam had lost the earth to Satan.

Exodus 19:4-7 Ye have seen what I did unto the Egyptians, and how I bare you on eagles' wings, and brought you unto myself. (5) Now therefore, if ye will obey my voice indeed, and keep my covenant, then ye shall be a peculiar treasure unto me above all people: for all the earth is mine: (6) And ye shall be unto me a kingdom of priests, and a holy nation. These are the words which thou shalt speak unto the children of Israel.

Twenty-five hundred years after the fall of Adam, God comes to Moses and uses him to deliver the Children of Israel from Egyptian bondage.

God brings the Children of Israel to Mt. Sinai and states: You have seen what I did to the Egyptians and I brought you unto myself. God is telling them "I am all powerful". He goes on to state if they obey His voice and keep His covenant they shall be a peculiar people unto Him. At the end of verse 5 God gets to the heart of the matter and proclaims "ALL THE EARTH IS MINE." This was said 2,500 years after the fall of Adam and therefore, the Churches' teachings regarding Adam losing ownership of the earth to Satan are unfounded. The earth belongs to God.

In verse 6, we find the reason for God revealing the earth belongs to Him. God states to the Children of Israel they shall be a Kingdom of Priests and a holy nation. God did not want to designate only one tribe to be His Kings and Priest, He wanted a Kingdom of Priests and a Holy Nation to rule and reign and take dominion over His earth like Adam was supposed to do (Gen. 1:26-18) but failed.

13

Although Israel failed to enter in and become that nation of Kings and Priests, God has accomplished His desire to have a Nation of Kings and Priests through His Church (2 Peter 2:9, Rev. 1:6). Every born again Believer is a King and a Priest and we are to reign on the earth (Rev. 5:10)… God's earth!

The following Scriptures will substantiate the fact this earth belongs to God.

Psalms 24:1 The earth is the LORD'S, and the fullness thereof; the world, and they that dwell therein.

David, who wrote this Psalm, did not believe the teachings that Adam lost this earth to Satan. He knew who the earth belonged to.

The writer of 1 Chronicles also concurs with David concerning the proper ownership of the earth and all that is in it.

1 Chronicles 29:11 Thine, O LORD, is the greatness, and the power, and the glory, and the victory, and the majesty: for all that is in the heaven and in the earth is thine; thine is the kingdom, O LORD, and thou art exalted as head above all.

All that is in the heavens and earth is thine the writer exclaims. The children of God need to understand and proclaim it with the same zeal and resolve as David and the writer of 1 Chronicles.

In the New Testament, the Apostle Paul gives his input on the matter. Paul, had the greatest revelation of Christ and his redemptive work. Jesus Himself, gave it to Paul. If you count Hebrews, Paul wrote 14 of the 21 epistles we have in the New Testament. Also, he influenced some of the writers of the other New Testament books.

1 Corinthians 10:26 For the earth is the Lord's, and the fullness thereof.

Paul knew the earth belonged to the Lord and that everything in it is His as well.

Some people will use logic that comes from outside of the Scriptures and assume this earth is Satan's. Some preachers say: "well, this earth must belong to Satan because look at all the devastation, the sickness and diseases, etc." All this proves is they know Satan is the source of devastation, sickness and diseases, etc., but are unaware he has been dethroned and we have authority over him, devastation, sickness and diseases.

We are to use our authority as Kings and Priests and heal the sick, cast out demons and bring peace and comfort to the hurting.

This earth belongs to God and He is waiting for His Royal Priesthood, the Body of Christ to rise up and take dominion.

CHAPTER 3

WHO'S LEFT BEHIND...
THE WICKED OR THE RIGHTEOUS?

Now that we know who the earth belongs to, let us now answer the question, who is going to be taken and who is going to be left behind?

In the book of Proverbs, we see a clear statement that precisely answers this question for us.

Proverbs 2:21-22 For the upright shall dwell in the land, and the perfect shall remain in it. (22) But the wicked shall be cut off from the earth, and the transgressors shall be rooted out of it.

These two verses are telling us that the righteous shall be left behind but the wicked will be taken out and removed from the earth.

Already, we are seeing the Bible contradict the popular teachings taught by the "Left Behind" books and movies.

I always use the rule, let everything be established out of the mouth of two or three witnesses. So, we need to see if there is confirmation to Proverbs 2:21-22.

Proverbs 10:30 The righteous shall never be removed: but the wicked shall not inhabit the earth.

What a powerful statement, the righteous shall NEVER be

removed. This is another open rebuke to the idea that the righteous shall be removed due to a rapture; therefore, we can know with confidence that we, the righteous, will not be raptured out.

Who is leaving? According to Proverbs 2:21-22 and Proverbs 10:30 the wicked are leaving. The wicked will not inhabit the earth because ultimately, they will be removed through judgment.

In Chapter Two, David knew God was the one who owns the earth. In this chapter we will identify David's belief on "Who Will Be Taken And Who Will Be Left Behind"

Psalms 37:9 For evildoers shall be cut off: but those that wait upon the LORD, they shall inherit the earth.

The evil doer will be cut off but the righteous shall inherit the earth. David seems to be in agreement with what is written in Proverbs.

Psalms 37:11 But the meek shall inherit the earth; and shall delight themselves in the abundance of peace.

Psalms 37:22 For such be blessed of him shall inherit the earth; and they that be cursed of him shall be cut off.

Those who are meek and those who are blessed, shall inherit the earth. This is talking about those who are in the covenant with God. Believers shall inherit the earth.

Those who are not in a covenant with God are called cursed and will be cut off from the earth.

Psalms 37:29 The righteous shall inherit the land, and dwell therein forever.

The righteous shall inherit the land and dwell therein forever. Never shall the righteous be removed but the sinful, shall surely be cut off from the earth.

Psalms 119:119 Thou put away all the wicked of the earth like dross: therefore I love thy testimonies.

God's answer to Job gives this eternal truth concerning the destiny of the wicked.

Job 38:12-13 Hast thou commanded the morning since thy days; and caused the dayspring to know his place; (13) That it might take hold of the ends of the earth, that the wicked might be shaken out of it?

The Old Testament states the ones who are taken are the wicked and the ones who are left behind are the righteous.

God's plan for the wicked is very clear. He is going to remove them from the earth in judgment and He is going to allow the righteous to inherit the earth and dwell in it forever.

We will verify if the New Testament is in agreement with the Old Testament on the ones who are left behind.

The greatest teacher in the Bible is obviously Jesus. What does He think about this matter? If we were to ask Him who's taken and who's left behind, what would He say?

Matthew 5:5 Blessed are the meek: for they shall inherit the earth.

This verse comes from what is known as the Sermon on the Mount and therefore, many people are familiar with it and have studied it or at least heard it a time or two.

I remember as a child growing up, every time I would read or hear this verse, I would think to myself "I thought the wicked was going to stay here and we were going to heaven in the rapture. Why does it say the righteous will inherit the earth?"

Now I know the answer to that question. It is because the wicked are the ones that are going to be removed and we, who are righteous in Christ, are going to inherit the earth.

Jesus knew the full implication of what He was saying because He was quoting from Psalms 37 which gives us great detail about the removal of the wicked and the permanent dwelling of the Saints on the earth.

Jesus doesn't stop there, He teaches the same throughout His parables.

Mat 13:24-30 Another parable put he forth unto them, saying, The kingdom of heaven is likened unto a man which sowed good seed in his field: (25) But while men slept, his enemy came and sowed tares among the wheat, and went his way. (26) But when the blade was sprung up, and brought forth fruit, then appeared the tares also. (27) So the servants of the householder came and said unto him, Sir, didst not thou sow good seed in thy field? from whence then hath it tares? (28) He said unto them, An enemy hath done this. The servants said unto him, Wilt thou then that we go and gather them up? (29) But he said, Nay; lest while ye gather up the tares, ye root up also the wheat with them. (30) Let both grow together until the harvest: and in the time of harvest I will say to the reapers, Gather ye together first the tares, and bind them in bundles to burn them: but gather the wheat into my barn.

Here, the tares represent the wicked and the wheat represent the righteous. They are both in the world and are growing together. At the end of the world which is the time of harvest, the tares are plucked, rooted out from the field and destroyed by the fire of God's judgment, just like it says in Proverbs 2:21-22 and the righteous are gathered into the householder's barn which is on the earth. In other words, the righteous, remained on the earth.

Jesus explains this parable to His disciples.

Mat 13:36-43 Then Jesus sent the multitude away, and went into the house: and his disciples came unto him, saying, Declare unto us the parable of the tares of the field. (37) He answered and said unto them, He that soweth the good seed is the Son of man; (38) The field is the world; the good seed are the children of the kingdom; but the tares are the children of the wicked one; (39) The enemy that sowed them is the devil; the harvest is the end of the world; and the reapers are the angels. (40) As therefore the tares are gathered and burned in the fire; so shall it be in the end of this world. (41) The Son of man shall send forth his angels, and they shall gather out of his kingdom all things that offend, and them which do iniquity; (42) And shall cast them into a furnace of fire: there shall be wailing and gnashing of teeth. (43) Then shall the righteous shine forth as the sun in the kingdom of their Father. Who hath ears to hear, let him hear.

Jesus says in the world there currently lives the Children of the Kingdom and the children of the wicked one. They will reside together until the harvest at the end of the world. In verse 40 He says that He will gather "out of" His Kingdom all things that offend. Remember, in Chapter 1 we noted that the Kingdom came to earth on the day of Pentecost and our job is to expand it through the fulfilling of the Great Commission. As nations are discipled, His Kingdom is exalted and fills the earth.

Jesus says He will gather out of His Kingdom here on earth all things that offend. He is talking about the wicked and their ways. He goes on to say the wicked shall be cast into the furnace of fire and the righteous will shine forth as the sun in God's Kingdom.

Jesus did not say the righteous were going to be removed, but they would at that time, simply shine forth in His Kingdom. He did say however, that the wicked were going to be removed by being plucked up and cast into the furnace.

Jesus continues with His consistent message of the wicked being taken and the righteous being left behind.

One of the most popular verses when it comes to the rapture is in Matthew chapter 24 and this is where the phrase one taken and one left behind originated. Yes, this is the inspiration for the "Left Behind" books and movies. The "so called" rapture that is taught from this verse does not exist.

Mat 24:36-42 But of that day and hour knows no man, not the angels of heaven, but my Father only. (37) But as the days of Noah were, so shall also the coming of the Son of man be. (38) For as in the days that were before the flood they were eating and drinking, marrying and giving in marriage, until the day that Noah entered into the ark, (39) And they knew not until the flood came, and took them all away; so shall also the coming of the Son of man be. (40) Then shall two be in the field; the one shall be taken, and the other left. (41) Two women shall be grinding at the mill; the one shall be taken, and the other left. (42) Watch therefore: for ye know not what hour your Lord doth come.

Context is the key to properly interpreting this portion of Scripture. You will notice there are two sets of people that are being described here. One being the wicked and the second being the righteous.

The wicked are described as "They and Them". The righteous is Noah and his family and Jesus refers to the righteous by calling the righteous Noah.

Jesus states in verse 37, as it was in the days of Noah, so shall it be in the coming of the son of man. He goes on to say that they (The Wicked) were eating and drinking, marrying and giving in marriage, until the day that Noah entered the Ark. Verse 39 states they (The Wicked) knew not until the flood came and took them all (all the wicked) away.

Noah knew the flood was coming and that is why he entered the ark. The wicked did not know until it was too late and the flood came and took them away.

Luke 17:27 They did eat, they drank, they married wives, they were given in marriage, until the day that Noah entered into the ark, and the flood came, and destroyed them all.

22

In Luke it is very clear they (The Wicked) did not know until the flood came and destroyed them all.

This is consistent with everything we have read in the Old and New Testament. The wicked will be taken away and destroyed in judgment. Therefore, when we read Matthew 24:36-42 we know "one taken and one left behind" means the wicked will be taken and the righteous will be left behind.

Because of all the wrong teachings Christian's have been saying "I don't want to be left behind" but the reality is, you don't want to be taken away and destroyed in judgment.

Jesus prayed a specific prayer for us in John. He is not wanting us to be taken out of the world in the judgment.

John 17:15 I pray not that thou shouldest take them out of the world, but that thou shouldest keep them from the evil one.

Jesus is praying for us not to be removed but that we should be kept safe from the evil one. This was before He went to the cross and stripped Satan of all his authority and placed him underneath our feet.

Now, not only is Jesus' prayer answered because God is not taking us out of the world, but also because Satan is defeated in our lives and we can rule and reign on the earth.

Revelation 5:9-10 And they sung a new song, saying, Thou art worthy to take the book, and to open the seals thereof: for thou wast slain, and hast redeemed us to God by thy blood out of every kindred, and tongue, and people, and nation; (10) And hast made us unto our God kings and priests; and we shall reign on the earth.

God redeemed us with the Blood of Christ, placed us in His Kingdom, placed Satan underneath our feet and now calls us to rule and reign in the earth.

So to answer the question of who's taken and who's left behind, the wicked are taken and destroyed in judgement while the righteous are left behind to inherit the earth.

CHAPTER 4

WHAT ABOUT THE RAPTURE?

What about the rapture? That is the big question. With all the buzz around the "Left Behind" books and the fear and excitement generated by end time prophecy preachers who teach the rapture, this question definitely needs to be answered.

Many Churches in America and other parts of the world are directly influenced by this teaching. So much of how the Church thinks, acts and lives today, is the direct result of believing this end time theory of leaving the earth.

If those who follow Christ believe that this earth is getting worse and there is nothing that they can do about it but wait for Jesus to rescue them, then that's exactly what they will do.

This defeatist mentality will reflect in every nation that the rapture is taught. As a result the Christians will withdraw from the public arena and give the affairs of this world over to wicked people who neither fear nor regard God.

As those wicked leaders drive our nations farther away from God and deeper into darkness and sin, Christians will respond by saying, "the prophecies are true, this world is getting worse and worse. Jesus come and rescue us." We will be quick to abandon the mission (The Great Commission) and retreat.

God's plan is not for His Church to abandon the mission and retreat, but to rule and reign through the preaching and teaching of the Gospel of Jesus Christ. As Believers save and disciple the lost, they will witness darkness being defeated and the light of Jesus Christ exerting its dominion.

We have already witnessed two powerful truths that changes everything. First, we eradicated the lie that says that this earth belongs to Satan. The truth has clearly revealed that the earth and everything in it, belongs to God.

Second, we witness as the Scriptures declared that the wicked will be judged and removed from the earth and the righteous will remain. As Jesus stated in Matthew 5:5 "The meek shall inherit the earth." Why is it that the meek will inherit the earth? Simply, it is because the earth, as God declared in Exodus 19:5, belongs to Him and He has a plan for it.

If God owns the earth, the wicked are going to be removed through Judgment, the righteous will inherit the earth, what about the rapture Scriptures?

A person might be thinking since there are so many Bible verses regarding the rapture, there is no way to disprove it. Actually, there is only one verse people might mistake for a teaching of the rapture.

The overwhelming majority of verses people use to teach the rapture are not even in the same ball park. It is simply absurd to consider them to be teaching or referring to the rapture.

Remember a good rule of thumb to consider when studying from the Bible, is to let everything be established out of the mouth of two or three witnesses. The following four Scriptures will support this rule:

Genesis 41:32 And for that the dream was doubled unto Pharaoh twice; it is because the thing is established by God, and God will shortly bring it to pass.

God established this message to pharaoh through a dream by giving it to him two times.

Job 33:14 For God speaketh once, yea twice, yet man perceiveth it not.

This is the reason that God establishes things by the mouth of two or three witnesses. It is because man often times does not get it if told once, or maybe even twice. Also, there is protection in more than one witness as we see in the next two verses.

Deuteronomy 17:6 At the mouth of two witnesses, or three witnesses, shall he that is worthy of death be put to death; but at the mouth of one witness he shall not be put to death.

God states if someone is going to pay such a severe price for a crime the basis must be from multiple witnesses, not hearsay, rumors or speculation from one person. This creates a secure safeguard for everyone involved and it will also create a safeguard for the messages we preach or that are preached to us.

2 Corinthians 13:1 This is the third time I am coming to you. In the mouth of two or three witnesses shall every word be established.

Let every word be established by multiple witnesses. Do not take one lone verse and try to make a doctrine out of it. This is the very thing that those who espouse the rapture teaching are doing.

The rapture teaching assumes when Jesus comes He will physically remove every Christian from the earth and deliver them to heaven. Now in order to validate such a claim, there should be at least two or three verses that clearly states God's removal of Christians from earth to heaven. Can you think of at least three verses to confirm the rapture teachings?

If you think you have found one verse, it could possibly be 1 Thessalonians 4:16-17.

1 Thessalonians 4:16-17 (16) For the Lord himself shall descend from heaven with a shout, with the voice of the archangel, and with the trump of God: and the dead in Christ shall rise first: (17) Then we which are alive and remain shall be caught up together with them in the clouds, to meet the Lord in the air: and so shall we ever be with the Lord.

This verse sounds like the teachings of the rapture, but once we explain in context, this will line up with the rest of the Bible verses which state, the wicked will be removed and the righteous are left behind to inherit the earth.

We will look at this and the other verses that those who teach the rapture so often use. But first, consider this… if the above statement in 1 Thessalonians 4:16-17 could not be explained away. Is this justification to preach "Jesus is coming to rapture us and take us to heaven"? No, it most certainly is not. Remember, we must allow everything to be established out of the mouth of two or three witnesses.

We must be like the Bereans and search the Scriptures and see if the things that are preached be true.

Acts 17:10-11 And the brethren immediately sent away Paul and Silas by night unto Berea: who coming thither went into the synagogue of the Jews. (11) These were more noble than those in Thessalonica, in that they received the word with all readiness of mind, and searched the Scriptures daily, whether those things were so.

Paul proclaimed the truth of the Gospel to the Bereans and they just didn't say "Amen, that was good!" instead, they searched the Scriptures to see if Paul was being true to scriptural consistency. Notice, they searched the Scriptures not Scripture. They wanted confirmation from multiple Scriptures in order to establish the things Paul was preaching were Biblically correct.

We must do the same. A lot of preachers are telling their congregations what they think God said. That is a scary thing because God is not obligated to act on what we thought He said. If you told God "well, I was taught you were going to rapture us to heaven, that is why I abandoned the mission that Jesus gave us." This statement will not be a good excuse! We must be faithful to study the Scriptures so as not to find ourselves in that predicament. Amen?

CHAPTER 5

DOES THE BIBLE TEACH THE RAPTURE?

It is time to get to the heart of the matter and find out if the Bible really teaches the rapture. We are going to look at the verses that are repeatedly used by end time prophecy preachers to teach the rapture and determine if their eschatology can stand up to scriptural examination.

The verses I want to look at are:

Matthew 24:36-42

John 14:1-3

1 Corinthians 15:51-57

Philippians 3:20-21

1 Thessalonians 4:13-18

Revelation 4:1-2

When one finishes reading this section, they will understand it is impossible to teach the rapture from these Scriptures without forcing their own interpretation upon them.

In Chapter 3 we have already reviewed Matthew 24 with the famous "Left Behind" verses. We will reiterate what was stated and view a few more details which will establish the fact these verses do not teach a rapture.

MATTHEW 24 – ONE TAKEN, ONE LEFT BEHIND

Mat 24:36-42 But of that day and hour knoweth no man, no, not the angels of heaven, but my Father only. (37) But as the days of Noah were, so shall also the coming of the Son of man be. (38) For as in the days that were before the flood they were eating and drinking, marrying and giving in marriage, until the day that Noah entered into the ark, (39) And they knew not until the flood came, and took them all away; so shall also the coming of the Son of man be. (40) Then shall two be in the field; the one shall be taken, and the other left. (41) Two women shall be grinding at the mill; the one shall be taken, and the other left. (42) Watch therefore: for ye know not what hour your Lord doth come.

Context is the key to properly interpreting this portion of Scriptures. There are two sets of people being described here. One being the wicked and the second being the righteous. Therefore, the context is the wicked and the righteous in Noah's day.

The wicked are described as "They and Them". The righteous is Noah and his family and Jesus refers to the righteous by saying Noah.

Jesus states as it was in the days of Noah, so shall it be in the coming of the son of man. He goes on to say that they (the wicked) were eating and drinking and marrying and giving in marriage until the day that Noah entered the Ark. Verse 39 says they (the wicked) knew not until the flood came and took them all (the wicked) away.

Noah knew and that is why he entered the ark. The wicked did not know until it was too late and the flood came and took them away. Noah was preserved from judgment through the ark and inherited the earth. This is a picture of what will happen to us. As the wicked are destroyed out of this earth in judgment, we will be preserved in Christ to remain and inherit the earth.

The parallel text in the book of Luke clarifies the wicked were destroyed and taken in judgment and the righteous were left behind to inherit the earth.

Luke 17:27 They did eat, they drank, they married wives, they were given in marriage, until the day that Noah entered into the ark, and the flood came, and destroyed them all.

Luke clearly states they (the wicked) did not know until Noah entered into the Ark and the flood came and took them away by destroying them all.

The popular "Left Behind" books and movies advocate these verses teach the righteous are physically taken to heaven while the wicked are left behind. According to the context of these verses, the wicked are taken and destroyed in judgment while the righteous remain and inherit the earth; therefore, it is easy to see their assumptions are wrong.

These Bible verses do not teach the rapture.

JOHN 14 – I WILL COME AGAIN AND RECEIVE YOU UNTO MYSELF

John 14:1-3 Let not your heart be troubled: ye believe in God, believe also in me. (2) In my Father's house are many mansions: if it were not so, I would have told you. I go to prepare a place for you. (3) And if I go and prepare a place for you, I will come again, and receive you unto myself; that where I am, there ye may be also.

Another popular misconception is Jesus is teaching the rapture in John chapter fourteen. In the second verse of John fourteen, Jesus says "and if I go and prepare a place for you, I will come again, and receive you unto myself; that where I am, there ye may be also." This is often taught to mean Jesus is going to heaven to build us a mansion, and when He completes construction of our new lavish heavenly dwellings, He will come back and rapture us to heaven to live in them.

This scenario, no matter how pleasant it is to think about, is not what Jesus is teaching. A simple look at Biblical context and themes will easily reveal that Jesus is an allegory of an house with rooms to teach us a deeper spiritual truth.

In verse two, Jesus first starts off by saying in my Father's "house" are many mansions. I submit, as I will prove, that these mansions are not the luxury home consisting of thousands of square feet which we often see behind gated communities. No, Father's house, or mansion speaks of the individual members of the church in which the Father dwells. To prove this, we will investigate the first part of Jesus' statement "in my Father's house" and allow the Bible to define what or who is Father's house.

What is Father's House?

John 14:2 In my Father's house…

The subject of verse two in John fourteen is Father's house. If we can first understand what Jesus meant when He references Father's house, then we can more perfectly understand the "many mansions" statement, along with His promise to go and prepare a place for us and come again to receive us unto Himself.

So, what is Father's house? The answer to this question should be obvious to the average Christian, but because of the way this text has been taught, the answer surprisingly slips by. Christians by default, take this statement to mean that Father's house is heaven and in heaven Jesus is building mansions for us. We must be aware that nowhere in scripture is heaven called God's house. Heaven is called His throne but never God's house. Scripture however, clearly tells us what God's house is. Here are six portions of scripture that answer this question.

1 Corinthians 3:16-17 Know ye not that ye are the temple of God, and that the Spirit of God dwelleth in you? (17) If any man defile the temple of God, him shall God destroy; for the temple of God is holy, which temple ye are.

In the Old Testamnet, the temple is often called the house of God for God dwelt there. Even so, here in the New Testament God dwells in His Holy temple and we are that Holy Temple therefore we are God's House.

Ephesians 2:19-22 Now therefore ye are no more strangers and foreigners, but fellowcitizens with the saints, and of the household of God; (20) And are built upon the foundation of the apostles and prophets, Jesus Christ himself being the chief corner stone; (21) In whom all the building fitly framed together groweth unto an holy temple in the Lord: (22) In whom ye also are builded together for an habitation of God through the Spirit.

Here in Ephesians chapter two, Paul is telling us through our salvation experience, we who have been brought into the Household of God are being built into God's Holy habitation (house). He uses construction terms to describe us as a house being built on a foundation, and being framed together for the purpose of being God's habitation, God's house.

1 Peter 2:5 Ye also, as lively stones, are built up a spiritual house, an holy priesthood, to offer up spiritual sacrifices, acceptable to God by Jesus Christ.

Here Peter calls us God's house and uses the same construction descriptions of the Church as stones being built into God's house.

1 Peter 4:17 For the time is come that judgment must begin at the house of God: and if it first begin at us, what shall the end be of them that obey not the gospel of God?

Peter here states that judgement should begin at the house of God. He clarifies that he is talking about the Church by stating "and if it first begin at us" making it unmistakable that we are God's house.

Hebrews 3:6 But Christ as a son over his own house; whose house are we, if we hold fast the confidence and the rejoicing of the hope firm unto the end.

Hebrews 10:21 And having an high priest over the house of God;

We see here, the writer of Hebrews says in chapter three verse six, Christ is a son over His house, then says whose house we are. Then in chapter ten verse twenty-one he continues by saying Jesus is high priest over the house of God, speaking of the church.

Scripture makes it abundantly clear that the house of God is not heaven but the Church. With this truth concerning the identity of "Father's House" we now can understand that when Jesus said in my Father's house, He was referring to the Church of the Living God. What about the "many mansions?"

What are the Many Mansions?

I have heard numerous sermons proclaiming that mansions await for us on streets of gold. I can assure you, Jesus was not promising you a mansion in heaven, He was promising you something so much better.

To understand what this Greek word (μονη☐ monē) translated mansions means, let us look at the only other place in the Bible it is used.

John 14:23 Jesus answered and said unto him, If a man love me, he will keep my words: and my Father will love him, and we will come unto him, and make our abode with him.

Here in verse twenty-three the Greek word (μονη☐ monē) translated mansions in verse two, is translated abode. The definition for this Greek word according to Thayer's Greek Definitions is as follows:

μονη☐

monē

Thayer Definition:

1) a staying, abiding, dwelling, abode

2) to make an (one's) abode

3) metaphorically of the God the Holy Spirit indwelling believers

The true meaning of the Greek word (μονη☐ monē⁻) translated mansions is abode or dwelling place. As a matter of fact, many other Bible versions translate this word mansions as rooms, abodes, dwelling places, resting place or some other variation. The NIV translates it as follows:

John 14:2 My Father's house has many rooms; if that were not so, would I have told you that I am going there to prepare a place for you? (NIV).

The NIV in essence says "My Father's house (the Church) has many rooms (individuals) He dwells in. Jesus is using an allegory of an house with many rooms to describe the Church corporately and the many members of the Church as God's dwelling place.

Here is a small list of Bibles which translate mansions in some other variation as listed above.

Amplified Bible, Basic English Bible, Contemporary English Bible, Darby Translation, Easy to Read version, English Standard Version, Good News Bible, God's Word Translation, International Standard Version, Jubilee Bible, Lexham English Bible, Literal Translation Bible, New International Version, Revised Version, Tree of Life Version, The Scriptures 2009 Version, World English Bible just to name a few.

With this understanding, we can plainly see Jesus is saying in my Father's house (His Church) are many, not mansions but dwelling places. In my Father's House, Father's Church are many places or people in which He dwells. That's because the Church is comprised of many, many multitudes from every nation on this earth in whom Father God dwells. Father truly does have a big house.

Now that we have the correct understanding of the first part of Jesus' statement, we need to grasp the second part so that it is clear He is not referring to being taken away in the rapture.

John 14:1-3 Let not your heart be troubled: ye believe in God, believe also in me. (2) In my Father's house (Church) are many mansions (Dwelling Places): if it were not so, I would have told you. I go to prepare a place for you. (3) And if I go and prepare a place for you, I will come again, and receive you unto myself; that where I am, there ye may be also.

We must realize where Jesus said He was going. He is not primarily speaking of going to heaven, He is speaking of going to the Father. Jesus makes His destination known in verse twenty-eight and also when He is questioned by Thomas in verse five and six. Let us examine verse twenty-eight first, then we will turn our attention to Thomas's questioning in verses five and six.

John 14:28 Ye have heard how I said unto you, I go away, and come again unto you. If ye loved me, ye would rejoice, because I said, I go unto the Father: for my Father is greater than I.

Here in verse twenty-eight, Jesus reiterates the promise of verse two and three. He says "you have heard it said that I go away and come unto you." Then He immediately clarifies where it is

39

He is going by saying "I go unto the Father." The destination of Jesus clearly is the Father. Now, look at verse five and six and you will witness Jesus explaining where He is going to Thomas.

John 14:5-6 Thomas saith unto him, Lord, we know not whither thou goest; and how can we know the way? (6) Jesus saith unto him, I am the way, the truth, and the life: no man cometh unto the Father, but by me.

Thomas said we do not know where you are going nor do we know the way. Jesus quickly replies and gives him the answer to both of his statements. In verse six, Jesus tells him the destination (where I am going) is the Father and the way to the Father is through me. Why is the way to the Father through Christ? Because Jesus said "I go and prepare a place for you." Meaning I go and prepare a place for you "in the Father". He accomplished preparing a way to be in union with Father through His work of the cross. Jesus is saying, through my work on the cross, I am going to bring you to the Father. I am going to restore man's relationship with His creator.

The Father being the destination which Jesus was talking about, becomes even more obvious when we examine the last statement Jesus made in verse three.

John 14:3 And if I go and prepare a place for you, I will come again, and receive you unto myself; that where I am, there ye may be also.

Jesus says I will receive you unto myself that where "I AM" you may be also. Notice Jesus did not say, that where "I will be" no, He said where I am. Where was Jesus at that moment in time? The answer to this question is found in verse ten.

John 14:10 Believest thou not that I am in the Father, and the Father in me? the words that I speak unto you I speak not of myself: but the Father that dwelleth in me, he doeth the works.

Jesus makes it known that at that moment in time, He is "In The Father". Jesus is telling His disciples that He is going to the Father via His death and resurrection, and when He comes back in the person of the Holy Spirit (John 14:17-18) through their salvation experience, they will be brought into union with the Father, for they will be His house, His dwelling place (John 14:2-3).

This becomes one of Jesus' dominate themes in this discourse with His disciples which starts in John chapter fourteen and ends in chapter seventeen. Jesus wanted them to know that His master plan was to bring them into a "relationship" of being in (in union) with the Father as He was in (in union) with the Father. Examine the following verses.

John 14:20 At that day ye shall know that I am in my Father, and ye in me, and I in you.

John 14:23 Jesus answered and said unto him, If a man love me, he will keep my words: and my Father will love him, and we will come unto him, and make our abode with him.

In **John 15:1-8** Jesus tells His disciples that if they abide in Him they will bear much fruit. The pinnacle of this abiding in Him is bringing the Father glory.

In **John 15:9-10** Jesus continues and says as the Father has loved me I have loved you. If you keep my commandments, you abide in my love, as I have kept the Father's commandments and abide in His love. Here again we witness

41

this desire of Jesus to bring His disciples into this relationship that He has with the Father through their union with Him.

John 16:26-28 At that day ye shall ask in my name: and I say not unto you, that I will pray the Father for you: (27) For the Father himself loveth you, because ye have loved me, and have believed that I came out from God. (28) I came forth from the Father, and am come into the world: again, I leave the world, and go to the Father.

Again, here we see Jesus telling His disciples where He is going (to the Father) and His desire to bring them into this relationship that He has with the Father through their union with Him.

John 17:20-21 Neither pray I for these alone, but for them also which shall believe on me through their word; (21) That they all may be one; as thou, Father, art in me, and I in thee, that they also may be one in us: that the world may believe that thou hast sent me.

In verse twenty-one Jesus specifically prays that all who believe in Him may be one in Jesus and in the Father as Jesus himself is in the Father. He continues this petition in the next three verses.

John 17:22-24 And the glory which thou gavest me I have given them; that they may be one, even as we are one: (23) I in them, and thou in me, that they may be made perfect in one; and that the world may know that thou hast sent me, and hast loved them, as thou hast loved me. (24) Father, I will that they also, whom thou hast given me, be with me where I am; that they may behold my glory, which thou hast given me: for thou lovedst me before the foundation of the world.

In verse twenty-two and twenty-three Jesus prayed that they (His disciples and all who believe) may be one, in union with the Son and the Father. In verse twenty-four, Jesus prays the very promise He gave to the disciples in John 14:3 to "come again and receive them unto Himself that where I am, they may be also." He is not taking them to heaven, but to the Father that they may behold the glory of being in (one with) Christ and in (one with) the Father (John 17:22).

John fourteen has nothing to do with being raptured off to heaven to live in mansions. It instead, is a promise by Jesus Himself to His disciples and every believer (His Church) to make them into a dwelling place of God our Father, that we may be one with Him through Christ.

In my Father's house (His Church) are many mansions (individuals He dwells in) I go and prepare a place for you (in the Father through the cross) that where I am (in the Father) you may be also (in the Father).

It's that simple.

1 CORINTHIANS 15 – IN A BLINK OF AN EYE THE DEAD SHALL BE RAISED

Many preachers use a set of verses from 1 Corinthians 15 to teach the rapture. As a child growing up I listened as preachers would say "You better be ready, because it is going to happen in the blink of an eye. Before you can blink we will be raptured to heaven."

I remember on several occasions blinking my eyes to see how fast being raptured from earth to heaven would be. I would think "wow, it is going to be really fast." The image of a super-fast rocket would come to mind, and I would think, the speed of a rocket couldn't even compare to how fast our trip to heaven would be.

Is this what 1 Corinthians 15 is really saying? Are Christians going to blast off like a rocket to heaven in the blink of an eye? Is this really a Scripture promoting the rapture or is it talking about something else altogether?

In order to understand the meaning of this portion of Scripture, one must first understand the context of the whole chapter in which it was written. First, we shall read in full, the portion which the rapture preachers advocate teaches the rapture, then we will put it in context by gaining an understanding of what the whole chapter of 1 Corinthians 15 is all about.

1 Corinthians 15:51-57 Behold, I shew you a mystery; We shall not all sleep, but we shall all be changed, (52) In a moment, in the twinkling of an eye, at the last trump: for the trumpet shall sound, and the dead shall be raised incorruptible, and we shall be changed. (53) For this corruptible must put on incorruption, and this mortal must put on immortality. (54) So when this corruptible shall have put on incorruption, and this mortal shall have put on immortality, then shall be brought to pass the saying that is written, Death is swallowed up in victory. (55) O death, where is thy sting? O grave, where is thy victory? (56) The sting of death is sin; and the strength of sin is the law. (57) But thanks be to God, which giveth us the victory through our Lord Jesus Christ.

As we read through these verses, notice there is absolutely no mention of leaving earth and going to heaven. If a person says that there is such a statement, they are forcing their own interpretation onto the Scripture.

Notice the sequence of events:

1. The trump sounds
2. And at the sound of the trump we are changed in the blink of an eye (not raptured but changed from corruptible to incorruptible)
3. The dead are raised incorruptible (and made immortal and receive their glorified bodies)
4. We who are alive shall be changed (and made immortal and receive our glorified bodies)
5. Then shall be brought to pass the saying "oh death where is thy sting oh grave where is thy victory?"

In this sequence, there are no suggestions of a physical removal of Christians from the earth in a rapture. The verse states the dead shall be raised incorruptible and those who are alive shall be changed.

In verse 52, one might consider this is talking about a rapture; where we physically leave the earth and go to heaven. The verse states the dead are "raised" incorruptible, but in order for us to find out what the phrase "the dead are raised incorruptible" means, we will need to first understand the context of this whole chapter.

In other words, we need to understand what the whole chapter is talking about before we can properly interpret this portion of the chapter (1 Corinthians 15:51-57).

We will take a quick review through this chapter and establish the context.

In 1 Corinthians 15:1-4 we see Paul defining the Gospel as the death, burial and resurrection of Jesus.

In 1 Corinthians 15:5-9 Paul is saying the Gospel he preaches is valid because there are many witnesses to the resurrection of Jesus. This is very important because this sets and establishes the context of the whole chapter.

Here in these four verses (1 Corinthians 15:5-9) Paul makes the point there are many people who have seen Jesus after His resurrection and therefore verifies the resurrection of Christ and the resurrection of the dead is real.

This gives us the context that will be carried throughout the rest of this chapter which is Paul's defense and explanation of the resurrection of Christ and of the dead.

In 1 Corinthians 15:12 Paul asked, in light of all the witnesses of the resurrection, how can some say there is no resurrection of the dead?

In 1 Corinthians 15:12-34 Paul begins to defend the resurrection of Christ and of the dead.

In 1 Corinthians 15:35-58 Paul begins explaining the concept of the resurrection of the dead. In the midst of explaining the resurrection of the dead, we find the verses that so many people contribute to the rapture.

The context of these verses (1 Corinthians 15:51-57) are not talking about the rapture but the resurrection of the dead. Now, with the context established we can clearly see what Paul is talking about when he says the "dead shall be raised incorruptible."

Paul did not say the dead will be raised up to heaven, he said the dead will be raised incorruptible. In other words, the dead will be raised in resurrection power. This is the very language that Jesus used when He talked about the resurrection of the dead.

In John chapter 11 we read about the death of Lazarus. We find out that Lazarus was very sick and close to death. Jesus was in another town and by the time that Jesus had arrived to Lazarus' home, he had already been in the tomb for four days.

When Martha, Lazarus' sister heard that Jesus arrived, she ran out and told Him that if He was there with them, her brother would not have died. That is when Jesus started to speak to her about the resurrection of the dead.

John 11:20-25 Then Martha, as soon as she heard that Jesus was coming, went and met him: but Mary sat still in the house. (21) Then said Martha unto Jesus, Lord, if thou hadst been here, my brother had not died. (22) But I know, that even now, whatsoever thou wilt ask of God, God will give it thee. (23) Jesus saith unto her, Thy brother shall rise again. (24) Martha saith unto him, I know that he shall rise again in the resurrection at the last day. (25) Jesus said unto her, I am the resurrection, and the life: he that believeth in me, though he were dead, yet shall he live:

In verse 23 we see Jesus tell Martha that her bother shall rise from death. Jesus was talking about something that He was getting ready to do, but Martha thought that He was talking about the resurrection at the last day saying, I know he will rise in the resurrection. Jesus quickly corrects her and "raises"

Lazarus from the dead and Lazarus' feet never left the earth.

John 11:43-44 And when he thus had spoken, he cried with a loud voice, Lazarus, come forth. (44) And he that was dead came forth, bound hand and foot with graveclothes: and his face was bound about with a napkin. Jesus saith unto them, Loose him, and let him go.

This sheds perfect light on the meaning of 1 Corinthians 15:52 as it states the dead shall be "raised". Just like when Jesus said that Lazarus shall "rise", he was not talking about calling forth Lazarus from the tomb and sending him to heaven, no He was referring to raising him from death.

In the same way that Jesus uses the word "rise" to refer to resurrection, Paul likewise uses the word "raise" to refer to resurrection. Now with the context of 1 Corinthians chapter 15 established as resurrection and not rapture, this verifies no one is leaving the earth and going to heaven, but rather the dead shall be raised up from death incorruptible into resurrection life.

When will this happen?

The answer to "when will the resurrection occur?" is given earlier in this chapter in verses 21 through 26.

1 Corinthians 15:21-26 For since by man came death, by man came also the resurrection of the dead. (22) For as in Adam all die, even so in Christ shall all be made alive. (23) But every man in his own order: Christ the firstfruits; afterward they that are Christ's at his coming.

In verse 21 Paul writes, since death came by man (Adam in the garden, Rom. 5:12) by man came the resurrection of the dead

(Jesus Christ). In verse 22 He says as in Adam all died even so in Christ all shall be made alive. NOTE: Some people who believe that everyone is going to be saved (whether they believe in Christ or not) use this verse as proof. This false doctrine is called Universalism or Ultimate Reconciliation. Is this verse proof that all will be saved regardless if they believe in Christ or not? Absolutely not. These verses put specific criteria on who is going to be raised by Christ when He comes. These verses state "all" who are "in Christ" (verse 22) and who "belong to Him" (verse 23) will be raised. You become "in Christ" and "belong to Him" by being saved through faith in His atoning work (Eph. 2:8, Rom. 10:9-10, 2 Cor. 5:17, 1 Cor. 6:19-20, 1 Cor. 3:23).

These verses are saying only those who are in Christ and belong to Him will be raised. Be on guard and do not let anyone lead you astray regarding the salvation of man apart from faith in Christ and His atoning work. Now back to the question of when will the resurrection take place?

Verse 22 and 23 says those who are in Christ and belong to Him will be made alive at His Coming. Therefore, according to these verses (22, 23) when Christ comes back, the resurrection of 1 Corinthians 15:51-57 will take place. Now we know the resurrection of the dead and living Saints take place when Christ returns.

Note the sequence of events; first, Christ comes back and second, the resurrection of the dead and living Saints take place, now notice what happens next. As we read on from verses 22 and 23, take note of the climactic event described by verses 24, 25 and 26.

1 Corinthians 15:24-26 Then cometh the end, when he shall have delivered up the kingdom to God, even the Father; when he shall have put down all rule and all authority and power. (25) For he must reign, till he hath put all enemies under his feet. (26) The last enemy that shall be destroyed is death.

After His coming and the subsequent resurrection of the dead and living Saints, verses 24-26 says, then comes the end when Christ delivers up the Kingdom to His Father, when He has put all enemies under His feet and the last enemy that will be destroyed is death, which is destroyed at His coming when He resurrects the dead and living Saints (1 Cor. 15:54-57).

Did you get that? Verse 24 says "then comes the end." This contradicts the popular thought (dispensational scheme) which teaches that after Christ comes back, Christians will be raptured to heaven for 7 years, then they will come back to the earth for 1000 years, then after the 1000 years, God will resurrect the wicked and they then will be judged.

No, it all ends right here when He comes back in resurrection power. It is at this time that the wicked and the righteous are raised together. The resurrection of the just and unjust are not separated by a 1000 years like the rapture preachers teach. Look at when Jesus says that these resurrections (the resurrection of the just and unjust) will take place.

John 5:28-29 Marvel not at this: for the hour is coming, in the which all that are in the graves shall hear his voice, (29) And shall come forth; they that have done good, unto the resurrection of life; and they that have done evil, unto the resurrection of damnation.

Jesus says the "HOUR" (a single point in time) is coming when

"ALL"(the just and unjust) who are in their graves shall hear His voice, and shall come forth (at one time), they that have done good (the righteous) unto the resurrection of life, and they that have done evil (the wicked) unto the resurrection of damnation.

Jesus, without a doubt, taught that when the righteous are raised, the wicked are raised as well. The reason why Paul does not mention the resurrection of the unjust here in 1 Corinthians 15, is because he is specifically talking about the resurrection of Believers who have died (1 Cor. 15:17-20), which as you will see, is the case with 1 Thessalonians 4 (1Thess. 4:13-14), but Paul, as Jesus did, believed that they both would be raised at the same time.

Paul makes this very clear in the book of Acts as He stands before governor Felix to plead his case, making a defense and refuting the accusations made toward him. Paul, after telling Felix that the charges are not true and cannot be proven, states he is really on trial for his faith and His hope in the resurrection. When he expounds on the resurrection he states the following:

Acts 24:15 And have hope toward God, which they themselves also allow, that there shall be a resurrection of the dead, both of the just and unjust.

Paul describes the resurrection of the dead not as a multiple event, but like Jesus a single event. He states there shall be "a" resurrection of "both" the just and the unjust. That is one resurrection, when both the just and the unjust are raised.

This is why Paul said "Then comes the end" when Jesus hands over the Kingdom to His Father, for He must reign until He puts all enemies under His feet and the last enemy to be destroyed is death, which takes place at the resurrection.

1 Corinthians 15 simply states when Jesus comes back, the Saints are going to be raised, the wicked judged and then comes the end.

No rapture is mentioned in these verses, instead we see the consistent theme that when Christ comes back the wicked will be judged and rooted out of the earth while we are changed, in a moment, in the twinkling of an eye, we will be raised incorruptible, as this corruptible puts on incorruption and this mortal puts on immortality, and we shall inherit the earth.

1 THESSALONIANS 4 – WE SHALL BE CAUGHT UP AND MEET THE LORD IN THE AIR

The verses in 1 Thessalonians 4 are probably the most quoted section of Scripture when it comes to attempting to prove or promote the rapture doctrine. At first glance and without context, it might seem that the rapture is what is being taught. However, we have discovered that we cannot rely on what something seems to say, like in the case of "One Taken and One Left Behind" without the proper immediate, scriptural context.

The people who teach the rapture say the righteous are taken and the wicked are left behind. If we were to look at those Scriptures (Matt. 24:37-42) based on their rapture theory, it would appear to confirm their opinion. However, as we have learned, the context of that phrase proves that not to be the case. The wicked are removed through judgment and the righteous are left behind to inherit the earth just like Noah.

As one investigates 1 Thessalonians 4, they must not jump to conclusions without properly considering the immediate scriptural context first.

1 Thessalonians 4:13-17 (13) But I would not have you to be ignorant, brethren, concerning them which are asleep, that ye sorrow not, even as others which have no hope. (14) For if we believe that Jesus died and rose again, even so them also which sleep in Jesus will God bring with him. (15) For this we say unto you by the word of the Lord, that we which are alive and remain unto the coming of the Lord shall not prevent them which are asleep. (16) For the Lord himself shall descend from heaven with a shout, with the voice of the archangel, and with the trump of God: and the dead in Christ shall rise first: (17) Then we which are alive and remain shall be caught up together with them in the clouds, to meet the Lord in the air: and so shall we ever be with the Lord

If you will note, there is no mention of going to heaven. If one assumes Paul is saying Jesus is coming to take us to heaven, they are making that assumption based on this statement in verse 17, "we which are alive and remain shall be caught up together with them in the clouds, to meet the Lord in the air".

They suppose the words "caught up" "clouds" and "air" mean or equate to leaving the earth and going to heaven. We can assume things, like most assume "one taken, one left" means the righteous are being raptured to heaven, but as we have seen, assumption without context often leaves us wrong.

It will be proven that the words "caught up" "clouds" and "air" do not mean or equate to leaving the earth and going to heaven. There are no black and white statements in these verses to justify the teaching of being physically raptured from one location to another. There are just three words (caught up, clouds and air) which gives us descriptions of something, but we must use context to determine the interpretation.

Paul here, like in 1 Corinthians 15 is talking about the resurrection of the dead. Take note that this is the very same language which he used in 1 Corinthians 15. The trumpet sounds, the dead are raised (not to heaven, but raised in resurrection power like John 11) and we are changed with them. By the language we can understand that Paul is talking about resurrection.

Also, more proof to establish the context of what Paul is saying is found at the beginning of verse 13.

In verse 13 Paul states I do not want you to be ignorant concerning those who sleep. We learn two lessons from verse 13. The first lesson is Paul establishes the context of this section as the resurrection of the dead (not the rapture). This becomes evident because he begins to talk about the Believers in Christ who have died and their subsequent resurrection from the dead.

To further prove this point, take note that Paul is using the same symbolic language to describe death and resurrection that Jesus used when He was talking about the death of Lazarus and his subsequent resurrection from the dead.

John 11:11-14 These things said he: and after that he saith unto them, Our friend Lazarus sleepeth; but I go, that I may awake him out of sleep. (12) Then said his disciples, Lord, if he sleep, he shall do well. (13) Howbeit Jesus spake of his death: but they thought that he had spoken of taking of rest in sleep. (14) Then said Jesus unto them plainly, Lazarus is dead.

Jesus tells His disciples that Lazarus is sleep and I must wake him. When His disciples did not understand what Jesus was trying to convey to them, Jesus plainly declared that Lazarus had died and I am going to raise him from the dead.

Just like Jesus, Paul is saying those who "sleep" or "are dead" in Christ will be resurrected from the dead just like Lazarus. Paul is clearly talking about the resurrection of the dead just like he was in 1 Corinthians 15. So the lens that we should be looking through to understand what is being said here, is not the rapture but the resurrection of the dead.

The second lesson we learn from verse 13 is Paul, from the onset of this topic of resurrection is using symbolic language. He uses the word "sleep" to give us greater understanding of the state of a Christian upon death.

When we sleep, we lay our heads down at night. But as sure as the sun rises on the next day, we shall rise up out of sleep with the sun. So it is with the Christian who dies in Christ, their spirit goes to be with Jesus in heaven (2 Cor. 5:8) and their body is laid to rest in the grave, but when the day of resurrection comes, they too will rise (or are caught up) out of death with the Son in resurrection power reuniting their new glorified body with their spirit.

We are not like them who have no hope, because we serve a Savior that has conquered death and because of that, those who die in Christ, shall rise again from death.

When we consider what "caught up" "clouds" and "air" mean,

understand, Paul like Jesus, is talking about the resurrection of the dead, using symbolic language.

We shall study these three words, caught up, clouds and air to determine their true symbolic meaning.

CAUGHT UP

The word "caught up" in Greek is "harpazō". The Strong's Concordance and Thayer's Greek Definitions references the word as follows:

Strong's Concordance

G726

harpazō

har-pad'-zo

From a derivative of G138; to seize (in various applications): - catch (away, up), pluck, pull, take (by force).

Thayer's Greek Definition:

G726

harpazō

Thayer Definition:

1) to seize, carry off by force

2) to seize on, claim for one's self eagerly

3) to snatch out or away

This word means to be caught up, to be seized, to be taken away etc. There is no mystery around the plain definition of this word. In the New Testament it is used 13 different times and is translated 6 different ways.

In every case this word is used, the subject never leaves the earth. There are however, two places where some say individuals left the earth and went to heaven but this simply is not true. The first place is found in Revelation 12:5, where the Sun clothed woman gave birth to the man-child and he was "caught up" to the throne of God.

This is not going from the earth to heaven, because the sun clothed woman was already in heaven when she gave birth (Rev. 12:1). She gave birth in heaven and the child was "caught up" or "taken" to God's throne.

The second place is found in 1 Corinthian 12:2, 4 where Paul was "caught up" and saw a revelation of heaven. He didn't know if his vision of heaven was in the body or out of the body but most likely, like John who received a vision of heaven, it was in the spirit (Rev. 4:2) and therefore, Paul most likely never left the earth.

In 1 Thessalonians 4, you will note catching up into the clouds does not involve leaving the earth.

Caught up is being used in the same sense that "rise" and "raised" is used by Paul in 1 Corinthians 15:52 and Jesus in John 11:23. Rise, raised or caught up, not from this earth but in resurrection power.

As one examines 1 Thessalonians 4:16-17 they will notice the word "rise" in verse 16 governs the interpretation for "caught up" in verse 17 by making a direct correlation between the two words.

1 Thessalonians 4:16-17 (16) For the Lord himself shall descend from heaven with a shout, with the voice of the archangel, and with the trump of God: and the dead in Christ shall rise first: (17) Then we which are alive and remain shall be caught up together with them in the clouds, to meet the Lord in the air: and so shall we ever be with the Lord.

Verse 16 states that the dead in Christ shall "rise". Verse 17 states we who are alive shall be "caught up" with them. Paul is conveying the meaning of rise in verse 16 to the word caught up in verse 17. Paul is saying we shall be caught up or risen with them. The question is, where are we going to be caught up or risen to?

Verse 17, states we who are alive and remain shall be caught up i.e. risen with them in the clouds. The verse does not mean we are going to be caught up in the rapture and taken to heaven, no, we are going to be caught up i.e. risen into the clouds.

Unless your idea of heaven is floating around on clouds and playing harps for eternity, you must understand, this is not talking about heaven.

We are caught up in the clouds, therefore, to understand what we are caught up or risen into, we must discover the meaning of clouds:

CLOUDS

If the clouds are not talking about heaven, what then, are these clouds that we are caught up in?

We will need to set the proper perspective of what we are reading. When Christ comes back in 1 Thessalonians 4 He is coming back with the clouds... what kind of clouds are these?

To find out, we must look at other verses concerning the coming of Christ that we may understand the Biblical pattern.

These clouds are not natural clouds. The Greek word for cloud and or clouds is "nephele" and is used 26 times in the New Testament and out of the 26 times, it is used to describe natural clouds only once. The word cloud or clouds most often are associated with God's presence and/or God's glory.

THE CLOUDS AS GOD'S PRESENCE AND GLORY

The cloud(s) often is used to refer to God's presence and/or His glory. Some example Scriptures are as follows:

Matthew 17:5 While he yet spake, behold, a bright cloud overshadowed them: and behold a voice out of the cloud, which said, This is my beloved Son, in whom I am well pleased; hear ye him.

The voice came out of the cloud that overshadowed them. This is not a natural cloud but a cloud of His presence and glory through which God spoke.

1 Corinthians 10:1-2 Moreover, brethren, I would not that ye should be ignorant, how that all our fathers were under the cloud, and all passed through the sea; (2) And were all baptized unto Moses in the cloud and in the sea;

You will note, this cloud is the glory cloud associated with Moses and the children of Israel in the wilderness. When the children of Israel saw that cloud, they didn't say "well we better get under cover because it looks like it's going to rain." No, they knew it was the manifest presence of God and it was a glorious sight. Numbers 14 states of this cloud that the Lord goes before them in the cloud.

Numbers 14:14 And they will tell it to the inhabitants of this land: for they have heard that thou LORD art among this people, that thou LORD art seen face to face, and that thy cloud standeth over them, and that thou goest before them, by day time in a pillar of a cloud, and in a pillar of fire by night.

Acts 1:9 And when he had spoken these things, while they beheld, he was taken up; and a cloud received him out of their sight.

In Acts 1:9 we see Jesus was taken up and received into the cloud. This is not a natural rain cloud, but rather it's a cloud of glory. How do we know that?

One way is by the "language depiction" which describes Christ relational position with the cloud as being "in it". When it says "the cloud received Him out of their sight" that is just another "language depiction" indicating the "glory cloud" as in Matthew 17:5 when the cloud "overshadowed them", Numbers 14:14

when the Lord goes before them "in the cloud" and the following verses (verses below) as when Jesus comes "in" the clouds and when they "entered" the cloud.

Another way we know it's not a natural rain cloud is because it says that He's coming back in like manner. So what we must do is look at the verses that talk about His coming and see what kind of clouds are associated with His coming(s). Let's look at the following verses.

Luke 21:27 And then shall they see the Son of man coming in a cloud with power and great glory.

Mark 13:26 And then shall they see the Son of man coming in the clouds with great power and glory.

The cloud(s) we see associated with Jesus' coming are not some kind of white puffy surf board but a cloud(s) of great power and glory.

Mark 14:62 And Jesus said, I am: and ye shall see the Son of man sitting on the right hand of power, and coming in the clouds of heaven.

Luke 9:34 While he thus spake, there came a cloud, and overshadowed them: and they feared as they entered into the cloud.

Acts 1:9 says that a cloud received Jesus out of their sight and His return will be in the same manner (Acts 1:8-10). According to the verses concerning His coming, He will be in a cloud of glory.

Luke 21:27, Mark 13:26 and Mark 14:63 states Jesus is coming "in" the clouds of glory. That is what 1 Thessalonians 4:17states about us. We are going to be caught up "in" the clouds.

Luke 9:34, states they entered the cloud and they did not leave the earth to experience entering into the cloud. Again, this is what we are going to do. When Jesus comes in His great glory, we will be caught up or risen (rise - John 11:23 or raised - 1 Cor. 15:52) together in the cloud i.e. the glory of His resurrection power.

THE CLOUDS AS THE DEAD IN CHRIST

Another way to understand the clouds that we are going to be caught up in, are the great cloud of witnesses.

Hebrews 12:1 Wherefore seeing we also are compassed about with so great a cloud of witnesses, let us lay aside every weight, and the sin which doth so easily beset us, and let us run with patience the race that is set before us

At the beginning of Hebrews chapter 12 we see Paul telling us we are compassed about with a great cloud of witnesses, who are cheering us on to run and finish our race. Who are the great cloud of witnesses Paul is referring to? If we go back to the end of chapter 11 we will find out.

Hebrews 11:39-40 And these all, having obtained a good report through faith, received not the promise: (40) God having provided some better thing for us, that they without us should not be made perfect.

Paul states, all these having obtained a good report... he goes on to state they without us should not be made perfect. And immediately after this, Paul informs us we are surrounded by a great cloud of witnesses who are cheering us on to finish the race (So that they can be made perfect with us - Heb. 11:40).

The great cloud of witnesses are the ones who obtained a good report. The ones who obtained a good report are all of the overcomers of Hebrews chapter 11. These are the faithful ones that kept the covenant, persevered and never wavered in their calling. These faithful ones are all dead and with God in heaven. Paul calls them a cloud of witnesses. This fits very well with those who are sleep (dead) in Christ in 1 Thessalonians 4:13-14.

1 Thessalonians 4:13-14 (13) But I would not have you to be ignorant, brethren, concerning them which are asleep, that ye sorrow not, even as others which have no hope. (14) For if we believe that Jesus died and rose again, even so them also which sleep in Jesus will God bring with him.

In verse 13 Paul is talking about those who sleep in Christ. Those who sleep in Christ are all the faithful Believers who have died and are presently with the Lord in heaven. In verse 14 Paul says when Christ comes back that He is not coming alone, but He is bringing with Him, those who have died and now reside in heaven with Him.

In Hebrews chapter 12 Paul refers to those who have died and are with God in heaven as the great cloud of witnesses. So Paul here is saying when Jesus Comes back, He will bring with Him those who sleep, or in other words, the great cloud of witnesses.

1 Thessalonians 4:13-18 is saying when Christ comes back, He is bringing with Him those who sleep which Paul refers to as the great cloud of witnesses. Then we who are alive and remain shall be caught up (rise - John 11:23 or raised - 1 Cor. 15:52)

together with them in the cloud of God's glory i.e. resurrection power and with the cloud of witnesses to be changed (be made perfected - Hebrews 11:40) and meet the Lord in the air.

So Christ is coming back and we will be caught up in His glory (resurrection power) with the other Believers who have died and gone to heaven (the great cloud of witnesses) and meet the Lord in the air. Does the word air signify that we are leaving the earth? A contextual investigation of this word will answer this question.

AIR

There are two separate Greek words translated "air" in the New Testament and they carry two different meanings. The first Greek word is "Ouranos" and the second Greek word is "Aēr". Examination of their meaning and implication will enable one to understand the true interpretation of its use in 1 Thessalonians 4:17.

The first Greek word "Ouranos".

Strong's Concordance defines this word as "The Sky" and "The abode of God".

Thayer's Greek Definitions defines this word as the following: "The aerial heavens or sky, the region where the clouds and the tempests gather, and where thunder and lightning are produced" also, "the region above the sidereal heavens, the seat of order of things eternal and consummately perfect where God dwells and other heavenly beings".

Strong's Concordance and Thayer's Greek Definitions both agree that this word "Ouranos" means "the sky, where there are natural clouds" and or "heaven, where God dwells".

This word is often translated as heaven, sky and air. Take note and see how this Greek word is used in Scripture.

Ouranos AS HEAVEN

Luke 10:20 Notwithstanding in this rejoice not, that the spirits are subject unto you; but rather rejoice, because your names are written in heaven.

Luke 11:16 And others, tempting him, sought of him a sign from heaven.

Ouranos AS SKY

Matthew 16:2 He answered and said unto them, When it is evening, ye say, It will be fair weather: for the sky is red.

Luke 12:56 Ye hypocrites, ye can discern the face of the sky and of the earth; but how is it that ye do not discern this time?

Ouranos AS AIR

Matthew 6:26 Behold the fowls of the air: for they sow not, neither do they reap, nor gather into barns; yet your heavenly Father feedeth them. Are ye not much better than they?

Mark 4:4 And it came to pass, as he sowed, some fell by the way side, and the fowls of the air came and devoured it up.

If it was this Greek word for "air" which means sky as in where birds fly and natural clouds are, or means heaven as in where God dwells, that was used in 1 Thessalonians 4:17, Paul would be saying that "meet the Lord in the air" meant that we were going to be caught up into the sky where the birds fly and natural clouds are, and whisked off to heaven as in where God dwells. However, this is not the Greek word that is used in this verse.

The word that is used in this verse is the second Greek word aēr. Let's review its meaning and implication.

The second Greek word "Aēr".

Strong's Concordance defines this word as "breathe unconsciously, that is, respire; by analogy to blow, air" and "circumambient or surrounding" meaning, the air we breathe that surrounds us i.e. the lower atmosphere.

Thayer's Greek Definitions defines this word as "the air, particularly the lower and denser air as distinguished from the higher and rarer air"

Strong's Concordance and Thayer's Greek Definitions both agree that this word "Aēr" means "breathe" and "the lower atmosphere where we breathe the air that surrounds us".

Please make a mental note of the above definitions. This word "air" is the "lower" air we breathe as distinguished from the "higher" and rarer air (as in where the natural clouds are or heaven).

In the New Testament this word is translated as air. Take note and see how this Greek word is used in Scripture.

Aēr AS AIR

Acts 22:23 And as they cried out, and cast off their clothes, and threw dust into the air,

1 Corinthians 14:9 So likewise ye, except ye utter by the tongue words easy to be understood, how shall it be known what is spoken? for you shall speak into the air.

In Acts 22:23 they threw dust into the air. That is right above their head. In 1 Corinthians 14:9 they spoke into the air. That is right in front of their faces. This Greek word Aēr is associated with the lower atmosphere that surrounds us. It is talking about here on earth in the place we are in.

We are not leaving the earth and going to heaven but rather Jesus is coming from heaven to earth and we will be caught up in or raised in resurrection power, in a great cloud of glory, with the great cloud of witnesses to meet the Lord in this air or our lower atmosphere that surrounds us here on the earth.

Yes, it is all going to take place here and this is exactly what 1 Thessalonians 4:13-17 is stating. Both Greek words for "air" are used here in this description of the resurrection. Now that we know the difference between the two Greek words, observe their use and meaning in these verses.

First, just to refresh your memory, here are the two Greek words for air and their meaning.

Ouranos - where the birds fly, clouds are, heaven

Aēr - lower atmosphere where we breathe

I will insert the two Greek words where they are used to help us better understand what is being said.

1 Thessalonians 4:16-17 (16) For the Lord himself shall descend from heaven (Ouranos) with a shout, with the voice of the archangel, and with the trump of God: and the dead in Christ shall rise first: (17) Then we which are alive and remain shall be caught up together with them in the clouds, to meet the Lord in the air (Aēr).

This is clearly saying that Jesus is coming back from heaven (Ouranos) to earth, this lower atmosphere (Aēr). And when He does, He is coming in great power and glory (Glory Clouds) and He is bringing all of those who have died in Christ (The Great Cloud of witnesses) with Him, and we all will be caught up or raised in resurrection power and death will be conquered forever.

Yes all of this takes place on the earth in our lower atmosphere.

There is so much more that could be written on 1 Thessalonians 4:13-17 but for now we will leave it there and move on to our next supposed rapture verse.

TITUS 2 – OUR BLESSED HOPE

From the book of Titus we get the term "our blessed hope" which many have come to interpret to mean the rapture. This is another major mistake of the Church. We have come to believe that "our blessed hope" is being raptured out of this earth and by so doing, we are blinded to the true blessed hope that this Scripture is referring to. Exploration of this verse will prove the rapture is not being taught here.

Titus 2:13 Looking for that blessed hope, and the glorious appearing of the great God and our Savior Jesus Christ;

There is absolutely no mention of the rapture. There is undeniably no mention of the Church being removed from this earth and taken into heaven.

This is mind boggling to see how impressionable the Church has become. This verse for example says nothing about a rapture or leaving the earth, and all we need is for some preacher to read this verse and with a little zeal and excitement exclaim "this is our blessed hope, when Christ comes back, He's going to rapture us out of here" which will be followed by a bunch of unquestioning Christians saying amen.

We know based on 1 Corinthians 15 that when Christ comes back the Saints are going to be raised, the wicked judged and then comes the end (1 Cor. 15:24). Christ is not coming back to take us out of here, He's coming back to consummate all things.

This verse says nothing about the Saints being taken away, it only mentions the appearing of Christ. Its message to us is "Our Blessed Hope" is not the going of the Saints, but the appearing of Christ. Why is the appearing of Christ our blessed hope? Because as we have learned in 1 Corinthians 15 and 1 Thessalonians 4, when Christ appears (or comes back) the Saints will be raised in resurrection power.

This also, is exactly what is being taught in our next supposed rapture verse.

PHILIPPIANS 3 – WE LOOK FOR THE SAVIOR

The next two verses allegedly has to do with looking for Christ to come back, rapture the Church to heaven and give them their new glorified bodies. Part of the assumption concerning the two verses is correct but the other part is very wrong. Let us review the verses to expose the wrong assumption made.

Philippians 3:20-21 For our citizenship is in heaven; from where also we look for the Savior, the Lord Jesus Christ: (21) Who shall change our vile body, that it may be fashioned like unto his glorious body, according to the working whereby he is able even to subdue all things unto himself.

There is no mention of the Church being taken to heaven. Instead, the verse states we are looking for the Savior to come from heaven and when He comes, He will change our vile body, that it may be fashioned like unto His glorious body, according to the working whereby He is able even to subdue all things unto Himself, which is resurrection power.

We are waiting for Jesus to come back and when He does, we will be raised in resurrection power. Remember our previous review on raised, raise, rise, risen or caught up, none were about leaving the earth, they were about being raised, raise, rise, risen or caught up in resurrection power (John 11:43, 1 Corinthians 15:51, 1 Thessalonians 4:16, 17) by which our bodies are changed and fashioned like unto His glorious body as corruption is swallowed up by incorruption, mortality swallowed up by immortality and death conquered forever!

This is why it is called "Our Blessed Hope" (Titus 2:13) and this is why we eagerly wait for Christ to come back.

REVELATION 4 – THE VOICE AS A TRUMPET SAID COME UP HITHER

In Revelation 4 there is an event which takes place that the rapture preachers say is the rapture of the Church. They state the trumpet blows and calls up John to heaven and this event must picture the rapture of the Church because from Revelation chapter 4 through chapter 22 the Church is not mentioned.

As one investigates their claim of a rapture in Revelation 4, they will be completely bewildered by their assumption that the trumpet blows, then the Church is raptured, because their proof is the Church is absent from chapter 4 to 22 which is simply not true.

The Church is very much present between chapter 4 to 22 and a quick word study will prove their rapture claim to be false.

Revelation 4:1-2 After this I looked, and, behold, a door was opened in heaven: and the first voice which I heard was as it were of a trumpet talking with me; which said, Come up hither, and I will shew thee things which must be hereafter. (2) And immediately I was in the spirit: and, behold, a throne was set in heaven, and one sat on the throne.

A door opens and John hears a voice as of a trumpet. This voice speaks and says to him "come up hither, and I will show you things which must be hereafter."

This trumpet voice invites John to heaven to show him things that will unfold. Notice, nowhere in these two verses is the

71

Church mentioned. This is a personal invitation to John alone for a very specific reason. If a person assumes this to be talking about the Church, they do it with no contextual evidence, and only out of pure speculation.

So the first point is this is an account of John being invited to heaven so he can be shown a specific vision. This is not a picture of the rapture of the Church.

Those who insist this is a picture of the rapture of the Church, try to justify their point by saying from here (Rev. 4) forward to chapter 22, the Church is missing from the earth and is not mentioned because they have been raptured to heaven.

They are concluding the word "Church" is not used in these chapters, because the Church was raptured.

How can anyone believe this line of thinking? It is very obvious to any person that is paying attention, the Church, between chapter 4 and chapter 22, is not missing. The Church is mentioned quite often and has a major role in what is going on in these chapters.

We know the Church is called by many names. Some of the names that we often hear are Saints and Martyrs who are Fellow Servants & Brethren. These names that equate to the Church are very much present between the chapters in question.

SAINTS

Throughout the New Testament Christians are called Saints. The following verses will establish this point.

1 Corinthians 1:2 Unto the Church of God which is at Corinth, to them that are sanctified in Christ Jesus, called to be Saints, with all that in every place call upon the name of Jesus Christ our Lord, both theirs and ours:

If you will note the language Paul uses "unto the Church of God" and "to them that are sanctified in Christ" these are the ones "called to be Saints."

According to this verse, Saints are sanctified Christians who make up the Church.

1 Corinthians 14:33 For God is not the author of confusion, but of peace, as in all Churches of the Saints.

Again we see the Church and the Saints are one in the same. The Saints are indeed present between chapters 4 and 22 in the book of Revelation.

Revelation 13:7-8 And it was given unto him to make war with the Saints, and to overcome them: and power was given him over all kindreds, and tongues, and nations. (8) And all that dwell upon the earth shall worship him, whose names are not written in the book of life of the Lamb slain from the foundation of the world.

Revelation 13:10 He that leadeth into captivity shall go into captivity: he that killeth with the sword must be killed with the sword. Here is the patience and the faith of the Saints.

Revelation 14:12-13 Here is the patience of the Saints: here are they that keep the commandments of God, and the faith of Jesus. (13) And I heard a voice from heaven saying unto me, Write, Blessed are the dead which die in the Lord from henceforth: Yea, saith the Spirit, that they may rest from their labours; and their works do follow them.

We see the Saints, which is the Church, are not raptured off into heaven but are present in the earth. Now notice Martyrs are present as well.

MARTYRS WHO ARE FELLOW SERVANTS AND BRETHREN

Stephen was the very first Christian martyr. We read about him in Acts 6:2 to Acts 8:2. Stephen was martyred by the Jewish leaders for his testimony of Jesus. The Bible tells how he was filled with the Spirit and did great wonders and miracles among the people of Israel.

Stephen was a Christian that was being obedient to the mission to save the lost, make disciples, heal the sick, etc. His ministry was so powerful and effective, that those of the synagogue, which is called the synagogue of the Libertines, Cyrenians, Alexandrians, and those from Cilicia and Asia, rose up and started disputing with him.

They started arguing with Stephen to disprove Jesus and thereby discredit his ministry. However, Stephen was filled with the Holy Spirit and the Spirit gave him such profound wisdom they could not stand against it and failed at their attempt to shut his ministry down.

The Century English Version's account of this reads:

But they were no match for Stephen, who spoke with the great wisdom that the Spirit gave him (CEV Acts 6:10).

This enraged them and they accused Stephen of blasphemy and eventually they took him outside of the temple and stoned him to death. This was the first account of a Christian giving his life for the name of Jesus and the cause of the Gospel. As a matter of fact, this was such a monumental and historic moment that even Jesus stood up in heaven to receive Stephen as he was martyred.

Psalms 116:15 Precious in the sight of the LORD is the death of his Saints.

God does not take the martyrdom of His Saints lightly. It is a very precious thing in the sight of God when one lays down their life for Jesus Christ.

This is the context of the Church that we see in the book of Revelation between the chapters, which those who teach the rapture, say the Church is missing because they have been raptured to heaven.

In Revelation chapter 6 after the supposed rapture in chapter 4, we find Christian brethren still on earth, serving the Lord like Stephen and preaching the Gospel of Jesus Christ.

Revelation 6:9-11 And when he had opened the fifth seal, I saw under the altar the souls of them that were slain for the word of God, and for the testimony which they held: (10) And they cried with a loud voice, saying, How long, O Lord, holy and true, dost thou not judge and avenge our blood on them that dwell on the earth? (11) And white robes were given unto every one of them; and it was said unto them, that they should rest yet for a little season, until their fellow servants also and their brethren, that should be killed as they were, should be fulfilled.

In verse 9 we see under the alter, the souls of the Christian Martyrs who were slain for preaching the word of God and for the testimony of Jesus which they held. In verse 10 these Martyrs cry out with a loud voice unto God and asked Him how long will it be until He will avenge their death? God answers them in verse 11 and tells them that He will avenge their death but first more of their fellow servants and their brethren should be Martyred as they were.

God is telling them that there are still Christians on the earth who are faithfully serving Him. These Scriptures are a testimony against this idea that there is a rapture in chapter 4 which removes the Church from the earth.

Now, therefore, this whole idea that Revelation chapter 4 teaches a rapture is incorrect. Let us summarize the following reasons:

First, the Church was not raptured from the earth but John alone went to heaven to receive a vision. Second, the notion that after chapter 4 through to chapter 22, the Church is missing from the earth due to the rapture, is absolutely incorrect. The Church is very much present in the earth between the chapters in question.

Conclusion? Revelation chapter 4, does not teach the rapture. Instead, Revelation Chapter 4, just like all the other Scriptures we reviewed, are misinterpreted by individuals who teach the rapture.

Where in the world do people get this idea of a rapture? We shall explore this question and find out.

CHAPTER 6

DID THE EARLY CHURCH FATHERS AND EARLY CHURCH TEACH THE RAPTURE?

The reason there is no rapture in Matthew 24, 1 Corinthians 15, 1 Thessalonians 4 or Revelation 4 is because the rapture doctrine is one of the newest doctrines that was invented within the last 185 years. The rapture doctrine was invented in the 19th century and before this time, no one from the 1st century to the 18th century has ever taught the rapture.

We shall take a brief trip through history to better understand the historic teachings of the Church and also, we will look at the roots of this false doctrine called the rapture and where it began.

EARLY CHURCH FATHERS & EARLY WRITINGS

Those who say the teaching of the rapture is something the Church has always preached and embraced are clearly mistaken. They often argue that the rapture was taught in the Bible by Jesus (Matthew 24), Paul (1 Corinthians 15, 1 Thessalonians 4) and John (Revelations 4) etc., and therefore, the early Church and the early Church fathers taught the rapture as well.

This assertion to prove the early Church and early Church fathers preached the rapture is a bad assumption, because as we clearly demonstrated, not one of those scriptural references are about the rapture.

Since we have previously demonstrated the Bible does not teach the rapture, they cannot say the Bible is proof the early Church and early Church fathers must have taught the rapture.

In order to know if they taught the rapture we must look at their writings and creeds.

As we look into what the early Church fathers wrote, please remember we are not exalting their writings to the place of Scripture. Also, while we are reviewing their writings, understand they are writing from a point of view that is free from the teachings of modern day end time rapture preachers.

They understood Biblical words like "caught up" to be related to the Biblical theme of the resurrection and not the rapture. Do not make the mistake of filtering their writings through the modern day rapture teaching but through a Biblical framework.

Irenaeus

Irenaeus (130 A.D. – 202 AD) was a bishop of the Church in Lyons, France. He was a disciple of Polycarp, who was a disciple of the Apostle John. Irenaeus is most-known for his five-volume treatise, Against Heresies, in which he exposed the false religions and cults of his day. On the topic of the Resurrection, in Against Heresies 5.29, he wrote:

"Those nations however, who did not of themselves raise up their eyes unto heaven, nor returned thanks to their Maker, nor wished to behold the light of truth, but who were like blind mice concealed in the depths of ignorance, the word justly reckons as waste water from a sink, and as the turning-weight of a balance— in fact, as nothing; Isaiah 40:15 so far useful and serviceable to the just, as stubble conduces towards the growth of the wheat, and its straw, by means of combustion, serves for working gold. And therefore, when in the end the Church shall be suddenly **caught up** from this, it is said, there shall be tribulation such as has not been since the beginning, neither shall be. Matthew 24:21 for this is the last contest of the righteous, in which, when they overcome they are **crowned with incorruption.**"

Because Irenaeus uses the word "caught up" the modern day prophecy teachers assume he must have been talking about the rapture. First, notice Irenaeus never mentioned leaving the earth and going to heaven. Second, as demonstrated, the words "caught up" deals specifically with the resurrection and means to be caught up in incorruption and immortality, which is to be engulfed by resurrection power and changed. This is exactly what Irenaeus was referring to.

Notice the last line, he starts by stating "for this." For this what? He is referring to the previous statement of being in tribulation when we are caught up. He then continues "for this is the last contest of the righteous, in which, when they overcome they are crowned with incorruption." The "caught up" that Irenaeus is referring to, is tied to the climax of his statement which is "crowned with incorruption." "Caught up" is the Church being crowned with incorruption. He clearly is referring to resurrection and this distinctly agrees with the definition of caught up set forth by the Scriptures.

If we could overlook the modern end time prophecy teachings and focus purely on the Biblical Scriptures, we can see Irenaeus is using a Biblical term. This Scripture refers to the resurrection and not to the Church being raptured off the earth into heaven.

Cyprian

Cyprian (200 AD – 258 AD) – Cyprian was Bishop of the Church in Carthage. During his short stint as leader of the Church, he guided the flock through intense persecution at the hands of the Roman Empire. In 258 AD after spending seven months of confinement to his home by order of Roman authorities, he was beheaded for his faith. Several of his works still exist today. One of which is "Treatise 7" whom many twist to teach the rapture.

"We who see that terrible things have begun, and know that still more terrible things are imminent, may regard it as the greatest advantage to depart from it as quickly as possible. Do you not give God thanks, do you not congratulate yourself, **that by an earlier departure you are taken away, and delivered from the shipwrecks and disasters that are imminent?** Let us greet the day which assigns each of us to his own home, which snatches us hence, and sets us free from the snares of the world and restores us to paradise and the kingdom."

The word they try to use to say Cyprian preached a rapture is "departure." He is not referring to the rapture, he is referring to departing in death. In fact the whole context of this treatise was to tell Christians that mortality and plague was not to be feared, because their "departure" from this world through death, leads to something better... Immortality.

The preceding verse (verse 24) verifies this by saying the following:

"**Laying aside the fear of death**, let us think on the immortality which follows. By this let us show ourselves to be what we believe, that we do not grieve over the departure of those dear to us, and that when the day of our summons shall arrive, we come without delay and without resistance to the Lord when He Himself calls us."

This "departure" is clearly not about the rapture but early death due to martyrdom, disease etc. The following quotes will identify to you that "departure by death" is what is being referred to in this writing.

"**Many of our people die in this mortality**, that is, many of our people are liberated from this world. This mortality, as it is a plague to Jews and Gentiles, and enemies of Christ, so it is a departure to salvation to God's servants." – Cyprian of Carthage, "Treatise 7, Section 15.

"**That in the meantime we die, we are passing over to immortality by death**; nor can eternal life follow, unless it should befall us to depart from this life. That is not an ending, but a transit, and, this journey of time being traversed, a passage to eternity." – Cyprian of Carthage, "Treatise 7, Section 22.

Cyprian's Treatise 7 is not talking about "departure" due to the rapture, but "departure" due to death.

Pseudo-Ephraim

There was a Christian named Ephrem or Ephraim the Syrian who died in the fourth century. The document in question "On the Last Times, the Anti-Christ, and the End of the World" is called Pseudo Epistle or "would be" Epistle. The reason it is called "Pseudo" is because there is much question concerning if the document was really the work of Ephraim the Syrian.

Regardless, the advocates of the rapture theory state this document teaches Christians would escape the tribulation through the rapture. As we have seen in the previous "out of context quotes" the rapture was a non-existent concept, and the early Christians were talking about something entirely different.

You will see the text in question states they escape through being gathered to the Lord not the rapture. Once we understand this point, we must then determine what the writer means by "being gathered and taken to the Lord." Is the writer referring to the rapture or is he talking about something else?

An examination of his writing will provide the answer.:

"We ought to understand thoroughly therefore, my brothers, **what is imminent or overhanging. Already there have been hunger and plagues, violent movements of nations and signs, which have been predicted by the Lord, they have already been fulfilled (consummated)**, and there is not other which remains, except the advent of the wicked one in the completion of the Roman kingdom. Why therefore are we occupied with worldly business, and why is our mind held fixed on the lusts of the world or on the anxieties of the ages? Why therefore do we not reject every care of worldly business, and why is our mind held fixed on the lusts of the world or on the anxieties of the ages? Why therefore do we not reject every care of earthly actions and prepare ourselves for the meeting of the Lord Christ, so that he may draw us from the confusion, which overwhelms all the world? Believe you me, dearest brother, because the coming (advent) of the Lord is nigh, believe you me, because the end of the world is at hand, believe me, because it is the very last time. Or do you not believe unless you see with your eyes? See to it that this sentence be not fulfilled among you of the prophet who declares: "Woe to those who desire to see the day of the Lord!" **For all the saints and elect of God are gathered, prior to the tribulation that is to come, and are taken to the Lord lest they see the confusion that is to overwhelm the world because of our sins.** And so, brothers most dear to me, it is the eleventh hour, and the end of the world comes to the harvest, and angels, armed and prepared, hold sickles in their hands, awaiting the empire of the Lord. And we think that the earth exists with blind infidelity, arriving at its downfall early. Commotions are brought forth, wars of diverse peoples and battles and incursions of the barbarians threaten, and our regions shall be desolated, and we neither become very much afraid of the report nor of the appearance, in order that we may at least do penance; because they hurl fear at us, and we do not wish to be changed, although we at least stand in need of penance for our actions!" – Section II

As you can see, the writer is telling and warning of the pressing tribulation. In the first sentence he states the coming tribulation was "imminent or overhanging." The writer believed they were on the threshold of great tribulation but the Lord would rescue them.

He gives hope to the Christians by telling them the following:

"For all the Saints and elect of God are gathered, prior to the tribulation that is to come, and are taken to the Lord lest they see the confusion that is to overwhelm the world because of our sins."

This is where the advocates get the idea that the writer is referring to the rapture. He says all the Saints and Elect of God are gathered prior to the tribulation and taken to the Lord. If you were to interpret this statement through the modern rapture teaching (which the early Church knew nothing about) and without reading any further, you would think this is talking about a removal from earth to heaven, but it is not.

All we have to do to prove this point is read a little further and we will see exactly what the writer is referring to.

"But those who wander through the deserts, fleeing from the face of the serpent, bend their knees to God, just as lambs to the adders of their mothers, being sustained by the salvation of the Lord, and while wandering in states of desertion, they eat herbs." – Section VIII

Notice they escape tribulation by fleeing from the face of the serpent into the dessert and bending their knees to God who will sustain them by the salvation of the Lord.

Obviously, when they are gathered to the Lord prior to tribulation, they are not removed from the earth but flee to the dessert, bend their knees to God and are sustained by the Salvation of the Lord.

Also, those who insist this is talking about the rapture say the writer is insisting that God did this so the Saints do not have to go through this tribulation. However, the writer believes that Christians will go through this tribulation. In the same document he writes the following:

"In those days people shall not be buried, neither Christian, nor heretic, neither Jew, nor pagan, because of fear and dread there is not one who buries them; because all people, while they are fleeing, ignore them." – Section IV

In those days. What days? The days of tribulation. He says in the days of tribulation no people will be buried. No Christians, no heretic etc. He is saying Christians, heretics, Jews and pagans are going to be dying but no one will stop to bury them because they all are too busy fleeing the dreadful tribulation.

Here is another example that proves the writer does not believe the Church was being taken to heaven, but would still be around in this tribulation. He further writes:

"Then, when this inevitability has overwhelmed all people, just and unjust, the just, so that they may be found good by their Lord; and indeed the unjust, so that they may be damned forever with their author the Devil" – Section IX

He says when this "inevitability" which is the pressing, imminent tribulation, has overwhelmed all people, just and unjust. He believes this tribulation would overwhelm the just (Christians) and unjust (Sinners) further proving the Christians were not removed from this earth to heaven in a rapture.

It is clear, if this document is authentic, that the writer truly believes they were in the end times and great tribulation was upon them. Therefore, he warns Christians about the pressing tribulation and adds comfort by telling them they will be gathered to the Lord and escape tribulation by fleeing to the dessert and bending their knee to God and being sustained by the Salvation of the Lord.

Again, there is absolutely no rapture mentioned.

The Apocalypse of Elijah

The Apocalypse of Elijah is an anonymous apocryphal work presenting itself as a revelation given by an angel. The title of this document comes from the mentions of "Elijah" within the text. Again those who hold to the teachings of the rapture try to use this and their proof that the rapture was taught before it was invented in the 19th century.

The text in question is found in Apocalypse of Elijah 5:1–6:

"On that day the Christ will pity those who are His own. And He will send from heaven his sixty-four thousand angels, each of whom has six wings. The sound will move heaven and earth when they give praise and glorify. Now those upon whose forehead the name of Christ is written and upon whose hand is the seal both the small and the great, **will be taken up upon their wings and lifted up before his wrath**. Then Gabriel and Uriel will become a pillar of light **leading them into the holy land**. It will be granted to them to eat from the tree of life. They will wear white garments and angels will watch over them. They will not thirst, nor will the son of lawlessness be able to prevail over them." – Apocalypse of Elijah 5:1–6

We read that Christians who have Christ's name written upon their forehead will be "taken up upon wings and lifted up" before His wrath. Since we read these phrases "taken up" and "lifted up" the rapture preachers say "the rapture was preached

85

before the 18 and 1900's." This again is desperation to try to prove a rapture doctrine that does not exist.

By reading the very next line their claim about a rapture is incorrect. The writing says they were taken up and lifted up on wings of angels, is this being raptured to heaven? No, this is not talking about being raptured to heaven. The text states once they were taken up on the wings of angels, they were "leading them into the Holy Land."

They were being lead to the Holy Land and not raptured to heaven. This is another example of failed claims of a rapture.

We shall review one more.

The History of Brother Dolcino

Brother Dolcino was the leader of the 14th century movement known as the Apostolic Brethren. An anonymous Latin document written in 1316 records firsthand information on the life and teachings of Brother Dolcino.

Yes, this is another attempt for the rapture teachers to prove their unscriptural theory of the rapture. In this document we must pay attention to exactly what is being said because as you will see, it has nothing to do with the rapture of the Church and everything to do with Brother Dolcino's strange teachings. Here is the writing in question:

"Again [Dolcino believed and preached and taught] that within those three years Dolcino himself and his followers will preach the coming of the Antichrist. And that the Antichrist was coming into this world within the bounds of the said three and a half years; and after he had come, **then he [Dolcino] and his followers would be transferred into Paradise, in which are Enoch and Elijah.** And in this way they will be preserved unharmed from the persecution of Antichrist. And that then Enoch and Elijah themselves would descend on the earth for the purpose of preaching [against] the Antichrist. Then they would be killed by him or by his servants, and thus Antichrist would reign for a long time. But when Antichrist is dead, **Dolcino himself, who then would be the holy pope, and his preserved followers, will descend on the earth, and will preach the right faith of Christ to all,** and will convert those who will be living then to the true faith of Jesus Christ."

If I was someone who taught the rapture, this would be the last document I would use to prove my supposed rapture theory. In the document it says that Brother Dolcino and his followers would be transferred into Paradise in which are Enoch and Elijah. They would remain in Paradise till the Anti-Christ is dead. Brother Dolcino would come back to the earth as the Pope, bringing his followers with him to preach the true Gospel and convert people to the true faith of Jesus Christ.

This has nothing to do with the rapture of the Church but rather just a "Transfer into Paradise of Brother Dolcino and his followers" only. Those who were transferred into Paradise (Brother Dolcino and his followers) would come back. Brother Dolcino as the Pope and his followers to assist him.

This is not teaching the rapture but instead it is just some weird belief that specifically pertained to Brother Dolcino and his followers only. No rapture taught, just a weird doctrine.

EARLY CHURCH CREEDS & CONFESSIONS

This view of the Church being raptured from earth to heaven has only been around since the 19th century and has never been preached by the early Christians, nor was it ever a part of any of the early Church creeds.

In this section we will look at the early Church creeds and prove that it was never a part of their theological or eschatological (end time) doctrine.

Note: If the creed is too long I will only reference the last part or the part that deals with eschatology (end time), otherwise I will place the whole writing.

The Nicene Creed (A.D. 325)

We believe in one God, the Father, the Almighty, maker of heaven and earth, of all that is, seen and unseen.

We believe in one Lord, Jesus Christ, the only Son of God, eternally begotten of the Father, God from God, Light from Light, true God from true God, begotten, not made, of one Being with the Father. Through him all things were made. For us and for our salvation he came down from heaven: by the power of the Holy Spirit he became incarnate from the Virgin Mary, and was made man. For our sake he was crucified under Pontius Pilate; he suffered death and was buried. On the third day he rose again in accordance with the Scriptures; he ascended into heaven and is seated at the right hand of the Father. He will come again in glory to judge the living and the dead, and his kingdom will have no end.

We believe in the Holy Spirit, the Lord, the giver of life, who proceeds from the Father. With the Father and the Son he is worshiped and glorified. He has spoken through the Prophets. We believe in one holy catholic and apostolic Church. We acknowledge one baptism for the forgiveness of sins. We look for the resurrection of the dead, and the life of the world to come. Amen.

Note: The word "catholic" with a lower case 'c' does not mean the Roman Catholic Church but the universal Christian Church as a whole.

The Chalcedonian Creed (451)

We, then, following the holy Fathers, all with one consent, teach men to confess one and the same Son, our Lord Jesus Christ, the same perfect in Godhead and also perfect in manhood; truly God and truly man, of a reasonable [rational] soul and body; consubstantial [co-essential] with the Father according to the Godhead, and consubstantial with us according to the Manhood; in all things like unto us, without sin; begotten before all ages of the Father according to the Godhead, and in these latter days, for us and for our salvation, born of the Virgin Mary, the Mother of God, according to the Manhood; one and the same Christ, Son, Lord, only begotten, to be acknowledged in two natures, inconfusedly, unchangeably, indivisibly, inseparably; the distinction of natures being by no means taken away by the union, but rather the property of each nature being preserved, and concurring in one Person and one Subsistence, not parted or divided into two persons, but one and the same Son, and only begotten, God the Word, the Lord Jesus Christ; as the prophets from the beginning [have declared] concerning Him, and the Lord Jesus Christ Himself has taught us, and the Creed of the holy Fathers has handed down to us.

The Athanasian Creed (500)

Note: The last portion of the creed is used.

…For as the rational soul and flesh is one man, so God and man is one Christ; who suffered for our salvation, descended into hell, rose again the third day from the dead. He ascended into heaven, He sits at the right hand of the Father, God Almighty, from whence He will come to judge the quick and the dead. At His coming all men will rise again with their bodies and shall give account for their own works. And they that have done good shall go into life everlasting; and they that have done evil into everlasting fire.

This is the catholic faith, which except a man believe faithfully, he cannot be saved.

Apostles' Creed (700-800)

I believe in God, the Father Almighty, the Creator of heaven and earth, and in Jesus Christ, His only Son, our Lord: Who was conceived of the Holy Spirit, born of the Virgin Mary, suffered under Pontius Pilate, was crucified, died, and was buried. He descended into hell.

The third day He arose again from the dead. He ascended into heaven and sits at the right hand of God the Father Almighty, whence He shall come to judge the living and the dead. I believe in the Holy Spirit, the holy catholic Church, the communion of Saints, the forgiveness of sins, the resurrection of the body, and life everlasting. Amen.

Note: The word "catholic" with a lower case 'c' does not mean the Roman Catholic Church but the universal Christian Church as a whole.

The Augsburg Confession (1530)

Note: Portion concerning the coming of Christ is used.

Also they teach that at the Consummation of the World Christ will appear for judgment and will raise up all the dead; He will give to the godly and elect eternal life and everlasting joys, but ungodly men and the devils He will condemn to be tormented without end.

The Canons of Dordt (1618-1619)

Note: Portion concerning the end is used.

SECOND HEAD: ARTICLE 8. For this was the sovereign counsel and most gracious will and purpose of God the Father that the quickening and saving efficacy of the most precious death of His Son should extend to all the elect, for bestowing upon them alone the gift of justifying faith, thereby to bring them infallibly to salvation; that is, it was the will of God that Christ by the blood of the cross, whereby He confirmed the new covenant, should effectually redeem out of every people, tribe, nation, and language, all those, and those only, who were from eternity chosen to salvation and given to Him by the Father; that He should confer upon them faith, which, together with all the other saving gifts of the Holy Spirit, He purchased for them by His death; should purge them from all sin, both original and actual, whether committed before or after believing; and having faithfully preserved them even to the end, should at last bring them, free from every spot and blemish, to the enjoyment of glory in His own presence forever.

The London Baptist Confession of Faith (1644)

Note. Only section XXXI is used.

That all Believers in the time of this life, are in a continual warfare, combat, and opposition against sin, self, the world, and the Devil, and liable to all manner of afflictions, tribulations, and persecutions, and so shall continue until Christ comes in His Kingdom, being predestined and appointed there unto; and whatsoever the Saints, any of them do possess or enjoy of God in this life, is only by faith.

Eph. 6:10-13; 2 Cor. 10:3; Rev. 2:9, 10

The Westminster Confession (1646)

Note: Only chapters (32 and 33) dealing with end time is used.

CHAPTER 32

Of the State of Man after Death, and of the Resurrection of the Dead

I. The bodies of men, after death, return to dust, and see corruption; but their souls (which neither die nor sleep), having an immortal subsistence, immediately return to God who gave them. The souls of the righteous, being then made perfect in holiness, are received into the highest heavens, where they behold the face of God in light and glory, waiting for the full redemption of their bodies; and the souls of the wicked are cast into hell, where they remain in torments and utter darkness, reserved to the judgment of the great day. Besides these two places for souls separated from their bodies, the Scripture acknowledges none.

II. At the last day, such as are found alive shall not die, but be changed: and all the dead shall be raised up with the self-same bodies, and none other, although with different qualities, which shall be united again to their souls forever.

III. The bodies of the unjust shall, by the power of Christ, be raised to dishonor; the bodies of the just, by his Spirit, to honor, and be made conformable to his own glorious body.

CHAPTER 33

Of the Last Judgment

I. God hath appointed a day, wherein he will judge the world in righteousness by Jesus Christ, to whom all power and judgment is given of the Father. In which day, not only the apostate angels shall be judged; but likewise all persons, that have lived upon earth, shall appear before the tribunal of Christ, to give an account of their thoughts, words, and deeds; and to receive according to what they have done in the body, whether good or evil.

II. The end of God's appointing this day, is for the manifestation of the glory of his mercy in the eternal salvation of the elect; and of his justice in the damnation of the reprobate, who are wicked and disobedient. For then shall the righteous go into everlasting life, and receive that fullness of joy and refreshing which shall come from the presence of the Lord: but the wicked, who know not God, and obey not the gospel of Jesus Christ, shall be cast into eternal torments, and punished with everlasting destruction from the presence of the Lord, and from the glory of his power.

III. As Christ would have us to be certainly persuaded that there shall be a day of judgment, both to deter all men from sin, and for the greater consolation of the godly in their adversity: so will he have that day unknown to men, that they may shake off all carnal security, and be always watchful, because they know not at what hour the Lord will come; and may be ever prepared to say, Come, Lord Jesus, come quickly. Amen.

The Methodist Articles of Religion (1784)

Note. Only Article III is used.

Article III — Of the Resurrection of Christ

"Christ did truly rise again from the dead, and took again his body, with all things appertaining to the perfection of man's nature, wherewith he ascended into heaven, and there sitteth until he return to judge all men at the last day."

As we reviewed the Church history and various creeds and

confessions, we did not see one single creed or confession mention anything about the rapture of the Church.

My question is. If the rapture was such a deeply held belief in the early Church, then why are none of the early Churches stating the rapture in their creed? Because the rapture doctrine made its ascendency in the 18th century and none of the earlier Christians or Church fathers had no knowledge of the rapture.

We shall turn our attention to the people who invented this doctrine known as the rapture and examine the roots.

CHAPTER 7

THE ROOTS OF THE RAPTURE DOCTRINE

Although no early Church father nor any of the early Church creeds and confessions mentioned, taught or even believed in the concept of the rapture, many of those alive today espouse that the teaching has been around since the birth of the Church.

They do this to try to counter the historic fact that this teaching of the rapture came about in the 19th century. It is very clear that this was a new teaching and was completely foreign to the historic Church and the Believers of that day. The great ministers of that time like Charles H. Spurgeon and George Muller, who are still highly respected today, rejected this strange new doctrine.

We have proved, this doctrine of the rapture, was non-existent for the first 1800 years of the Church, so now, let us review the roots and discover where the rapture came from.

Emmanuel Lucunza

A Jesuit priest named Emmanuel Lucunza (1731-1801) wrote a book called "The Coming of Messiah in Glory and Majesty" which some speculate, contained what are the first known allusions to a new concept called the rapture. Edward Irving, a

Scottish minister, discovered the book in London and was so impacted by the book that he translated it to English.

Edward Irving

Edward Irving (1792 -1834) was a Scottish minister associated with the origins of the Catholic Apostolic Church. He was a very magnetic speaker who drew massive crowds to his open air meetings and his Church.

Irving upon discovering Lucunza's book and being impacted by it, translated the work to English. At this time, Irvin's view of eschatology (end times) was changed and one of two scenarios took place. Either Irving received the impression that Lucunza was teaching the Saints would be removed from this earth through the rapture and fully embraced the new doctrine, or Lucunza's teachings did not leave Irving with the rapture impression and he would not conceive of the new doctrine until Margaret MacDonald's "vision". Regardless of which scenario, after 1830 Irving began a series of prophecy meetings and proclaimed these strange new teachings of Lucunza's publicly.

Along with these new concepts, Irving also started promoting several false teachings. One heretical teaching being Christ's human nature was sinful, which led Irving to be excommunicated by the presbytery in 1830, followed by a Church split in 1833 and his death due to sickness in 1834.

One individual that has been sourced as the creator of this new rapture doctrine that would be later preached by Edward Irving, was a young girl by the name of Margaret MacDonald.

Margaret MacDonald

In 1830 there was a young girl from Port Glasgow, Scotland, named Margaret MacDonald (1815-1840). She and her family were followers of Edward Irving and the Catholic Apostolic movement.

The movement was beginning to explore and emphasize charismatic gifts along with the new eschatological teachings. In 1830 MacDonald, fell into a trance and said that she received a vision of the Church being raptured into heaven.

It is not clear, if Irving received his teaching from Lucunza and influenced MacDonald or if Irving who was already influenced by Lucunza's teaching, received the rapture idea from Macdonald and added this to the new eschatological teaching he was already endorsing. Regardless, Margaret MacDonald along with Edward Irving became strong promoters of the rapture teaching and was sharing it with anyone who would listen.

As people began to adhere to this new outline of eschatology, there was no true clarity on the details of what was being proposed until a clerk from the Church of England named John Nelson Darby took this new teaching and added it to his own new system of dispensationalism.

John Nelson Darby

John Nelson Darby (1800-1882) Leader of the Plymouth Brethren Movement went to investigate the charismatic gifts along with the new eschatological teachings that were being promoted by Irving and his followers. As Darby attended the series of Bible Prophecy meetings he learned about the rapture and the visions of Margaret MacDonald. According to Dave

MacPherson who has thoroughly examined and written extensively on this topic, Darby, after attending the meetings, visited Margaret Macdonald in her home

Upon completing his investigation, John N. Darby rejected the charismatic expressions but embraced and started teaching the rapture theory promoted by Edward Irving and his followers. Darby became the chief advocate of this new teaching by preaching the rapture theory everywhere he went. It wasn't without resistance however, many of his own followers and associates departed from him. Also, many great men of God from the 1800's like George Muller (1805 – 1898), William Booth (1829 – 1912) and Charles Spurgeon (1834 – 1892) opposed Darby's teachings.

You may be wondering, if all this is true then how did this teaching get so popular? Darby, being a leader of the Plymouth Brethren Movement, started promoting the new doctrine. Through the Plymouth Brethren Movement a man named Cyrus Ingerson Scofield was exposed to this teaching and became one of its most influential advocates.

Cyrus Ingerson Scofield

C. I. Scofield (1843 – 1921) a Congregational preacher, learned of this new doctrine through the Plymouth Brethren Movement. Darby took several trips to America and made a powerful impact in developing the Plymouth Brethren Movement. It was through this movement that his views on the rapture spread and eventually caught the attention of Scofield.

Scofield became a fervent promoter of the new rapture teaching and in 1909 he incorporated Darby's notes into the footnotes of his new Scofield Reference Bible. One million copies were printed by 1930 and within the first fifty years over three million copies were published.

The Scofield Reference Bible was introduced to Bible schools all across America and the new rapture doctrine began to mold the minds of Bible students who became the next generation preachers; who then began to proclaim this false concept to the masses of America and beyond.

As a result, America has been highly influenced by this false doctrine even to the point that we are allowing the fruits of it to ruin our country. You may ask what I mean by that statement and how is it ruining our country?

As you observe American history, at the beginning, you will see a strong Christian emphasis in the public arena and in the home. We used to have Bibles in school. We used to pray in school. We used to allow the 10 commandments, crosses and nativity scenes on our public displays, courtyards and state capitals. We used to emphasize strong family values and high standards of righteousness. We used to stand against immoral actions and displays at home, in public and in politics.

However, with the increase of this new doctrine starting in 1909 and really taking off in the 1930's, we were taught this earth is getting worse and there is nothing we can do but wait for Jesus to rapture us out of here. Instead of standing against the immoral corruption we see at home, in public and politics, we started to slowly surrender and accept it as our fate because we began to think "well this is the way it is supposed to be." The result of this is we have immoral leaders who stand against God, promote everything ungodly and start to persecute the Church.

This my dear brothers and sisters, is what we are living in and is the result of this unbiblical teaching of the rapture.

Remember, this teaching is not taught in the Bible, nor was it taught by any of the early Church fathers, nor was it in any of the Church creeds and confessions but made its appearance in history at the end of the 18th and early 19th century starting possibly with Emmanuel Lucunza, definitely with Edward Irving, Margaret MacDonald, John Nelson Darby and C. I. Scofield.

Great men of God from Darby's time like George Muller, William Booth and Charles Spurgeon all rejected Darby's teaching and called them unscriptural. Also contemporaries of Scofield's time like Charles R. Erdman (1866-1960), A. J. Gordon (1836-1895) and W.G. Moorhead (1836-1914) rejected this strange new doctrine.

Furthermore, before the 1800's no prominent minister nor reformer like John Wycliffe (1331-1384), William Tyndale (1449–1536), Martin Luther (1483–1546), John Calvin (1509–1564), John Foxe (1516–1587), Isaac Newton (1643–1727) or John Wesley (1703–1791) ever taught such a thing.

The rapture theory is a completely false doctrine formed in the 1800's and has created a defeatist and escapist mentality in the Church.

Now is the time to reject such a doctrine and break the shackles of a defeatist and escapist mentally, take our place in society, reclaim our calling and bring the light of Christ to all nations by fulfilling the Great Commission.

CHAPTER 8

TAKING OUR PLACE IN SOCIETY

As I have already stated, the rapture doctrine has done more to harm the Church and to slow down the work of the Great Commission than nearly all the other futurist doctrines combined.

People have often argued because of the rapture they are more passionate to win souls. This may seem like good logic but we have already witnessed through American history that the false concept of the rapture, although it may inspire some Christians to be more passionate about winning souls, has overall caused the Church to adopt a defeatist and escapist mentality. As a byproduct, the Church has disengaged from the public arena and has turned control of our politics and culture over to the wicked. The Church has done this because we falsely believe it is supposed to be this way.

The Chinese Church experienced this same trap. Before the outbreak of communism in China, missionary work was flourishing and the Gospel was prevailing. The nation of China was being converted and discipled into Christianity. At that time this new western teaching of the rapture was introduced to the Chinese Church and they embraced it.

In 1947 Mao Tse Tung introduced communism to China. The western Christians who promoted the new rapture teaching, left China and intense persecution came upon the Chinese Church.

The worry and concern that gripped the Chinese Church was quickly put to rest as the Church leaders reminded everyone of this new western doctrine. The Church leaders told them they were not going to endure persecution, but will escape through the rapture.

Sadly, this proved to be wrong. Millions of Christians were tortured to death and the communist movement continued. As a result, over 70,000,000 Chinese people died.

The Chinese Church were taught the world was getting worse and there was nothing they could do but wait for Jesus to rapture them out of here. What if instead they were taught the truth? That God wanted them to disciple and raise up Godly Christian leaders that would get involved with the political and cultural affairs of China. Christian leaders who would shine God's light in those arenas.

Maybe they would have stopped the rise of communism in the first place and save the lives of over 70,000,000 Chinese people.

Make no mistake, God has called us to be completely engaged in our politics and culture in order to promote righteousness because as it is written "righteousness exalts a nation." Let us review some Scriptures.

Proverbs 14:34 Righteousness exalteth a nation: but sin is a reproach to any people.

Psalms 33:12 Blessed is the nation whose God is the LORD; and the people whom he hath chosen for his own inheritance.

Are not the above Scriptures eternal? Do they not mean anything to us today?

1 Peter 1:24-25 For all flesh is as grass, and all the glory of man as the flower of grass. The grass withereth, and the flower thereof falleth away: (25) But the word of the Lord endureth for ever. And this is the word which by the gospel is preached unto you.

Flesh is as grass and the glory of man shall fade away but the word of the LORD shall endure forever. God's word is eternal and ever relevant. What it meant back then is the very thing it means now.

Blessed is the nation whose God is the LORD. Why? Because righteousness, God's righteousness exalts a nation. God wants the people of America, and every other nation in the earth to make Him their Lord!

How do we do this? Do we elect leaders to legislate righteousness? Not really. We primarily change our nation by changing the heart of the people of the nation. And we change the heart of the people of a nation by sharing the Gospel with them to bring them into salvation, and then make disciples of them so that they may know, observe and follow all the teachings of Jesus Christ.

Matthew 28:19-20 Go ye therefore, and make disciples of all nations, baptizing them in the name of the Father, and of the Son, and of the Holy Ghost: (20) Teaching them to observe all things whatsoever I have commanded you: and, lo, I am with you always, even unto the end of the world. Amen.

When you change a person's heart from loving evil and hating righteousness to loving righteousness and hating evil, you will not have to pass a law that says this is evil so you cannot do it. Rather, the converted and discipled Christian, from the heart, will shun evil and cling to good.

Consider Old Testament Israel who had the perfect law (The Law of Moses) that governed their society. Even though they had the perfect law, they still rebelled against God because they had wicked hearts which rebelled against the righteousness of God's law. Therefore, in order for Israel to obey God's laws, they first must be converted in their hearts.

In this same way, unless we convert the hearts of the people who make up our nation, they will always rebel against righteous laws. This is the reason that the only way to really transform any nation is through the fulfillment of the Great Commission.

Does this mean we are to disengage from the public arena? No, we are to engage in every area of the public arena. We need to get involved and dominate all of the following arenas: business, government, media, arts and entertainment, education, the family and religion.

If you pull out the light of Christ from any of these arenas, they will become vehicles for sin, immorality and corruption to filter through. This will ultimately shape our culture and cause the hatred that exists towards Christ and His Church to take on a tangible form in various kinds of persecution.

One might say "I thought we are not to get involved with politics." My reply is, "What you heard is wrong and did not come from the Bible." The Bible is very clear God uses the governmental systems of this world to promote righteousness and punish evil.

One of the places in the Bible where people often make an argument that Christians are to just accept the "laws of the land" regardless if they are righteous laws or evil laws, is in Romans chapter 13.

I often hear the argument that it's the law of the land and Christians are just to accept it. My reply again, is if that law tries to get me or another Christian to violate what God has clearly stated in Scripture, then we must reject it. We must rise up and vote out of office those who defy God with their immoral law making. For one who governs must govern according to the righteous precepts of God's Word, for only then, do they uphold the purpose of their position. Note the following verse:

Proverbs 16:12-14 It is an abomination to kings to commit wickedness: for the throne is established by righteousness. (13) Righteous lips are the delight of kings; and they love him that speaketh right. (14) The wrath of a king is as messengers of death: but a wise man will pacify it.

God is not honored or pleased when a king commits wickedness because the throne is established in righteousness. When a king upholds the righteousness of God's precepts, God is pleased and honored. Only when he upholds the righteousness of God's precepts, will a king's wrath be a tool for God to punish wickedness.

Although many people use Romans 13 as a Biblical reason for Christians to just bow down and accept the wicked laws of the land, Romans 13 actually states the opposite and repeats the principals of Proverbs 16:12-14.

To understand Romans 13 we must start at the end of Romans Chapter 12. Remember, the book of Romans is a letter and originally has no chapter divisions. When Paul gets to the end of chapter 12 and starts on chapter 13, he does not change topics, but continues to elaborate on the subject.

Romans 12:17-21 Repay no one evil for evil, but give thought to do what is honorable in the sight of all. (18) If possible, so far as it depends on you, live peaceably with all. (19) Beloved, never avenge yourselves, but leave it to the wrath of God, for it is written, "Vengeance is mine, I will repay, says the Lord." (20) To the contrary, "if your enemy is hungry, feed him; if he is thirsty, give him something to drink; for by so doing you will heap burning coals on his head." (21) Do not be overcome by evil, but overcome evil with good.

Here we see Paul saying, when someone does evil to you, do not avenge yourself, but leave it to the wrath of God and He will repay, because vengeance belongs to God. Most assume what God is trying to tell us is "after the end comes, on the day of judgment, I will finally pay them back for all the wickedness that they have done to you."

So we think that God's vengeance and wrath has nothing to do with this lifetime. Our only response is to overcome evil by doing good back to them because one sweet day in the by and by, God will repay them for me.

This is partly right and partly wrong. The right part is we are to always do good to those who commit evil against us. Remember our ultimate goal is to see them come to saving faith in Jesus Christ and by doing good to them, we may save some.

The part that is wrong is the vengeance and wrath of God is not something that has to do with the judgment which takes place after Christ comes. This vengeance and wrath is God's way of punishing evil now, in our day and in our time. In order to understand this we must keep in mind the context of what we just read at the end of Chapter 12 and bring it into chapter 13.

Romans 13:1-5 Let every person be subject to the governing authorities. For there is no authority except from God, and those that exist have been instituted by God. (2) Therefore whoever resists the authorities resists what God has appointed, and those who resist will incur judgment. (3) For rulers are not a terror to good conduct, but to bad. Would you have no fear of the one who is in authority? Then do what is good, and you will receive his approval, (4) for he is God's servant for your good. But if you do wrong, be afraid, for he does not bear the sword in vain. For he is the servant of God, an avenger who carries out God's wrath on the wrongdoer. (5) Therefore one must be in subjection, not only to avoid God's wrath but also for the sake of conscience.

Verse 1 commands that every person must be subject to the governing authority because it is appointed by God. Then verse 2 says if you resist authority you are resisting God and will incur judgment.

Verse 3 states the ruler that God has appointed (verse 1), is not a terror against those who do good but it is a terror against those who do evil. Paul continues saying if you don't want to fear the rulers, then do good.

This is a very critical point for us to understand. This does not, in any way say all rulers are appointed by God. The rulers who are appointed by God do good and punish evil. This is the criteria for a God appointed ruler. If you see a ruler who disregards God's righteous precepts, than know for sure, that ruler is not appointed by God.

Do I believe God can raise up evil rulers for His own purpose? Yes I do believe and we have examples in the Bible of God doing that. This is usually the consequence of God's people rebelling from His ways and as a result evil rulers start to rule. If a nation follows His ways and appoints righteous rulers who govern according to the righteous precepts of God, the Bible says God will exalt that nation.

Remember Proverbs 16:12-14 says that God establishes a throne by righteousness. And when a king rules in righteousness, the king's wrath will be a tool for God to punish wickedness. This is exactly the point of what is being said in Romans 13.

Recall at the end of chapter 12 when God says do not avenge yourself because vengeance belongs to Him and He will repay? In chapter 13 He begins telling how He will repay. In verse 4 of chapter 13 Paul says the ruler appointed by God is God's avenger to carry out God's wrath on wrongdoers.

This is why He says don't avenge yourself. God is telling us that vengeance and wrath belongs to Him and through our governmental systems, He uses upright rulers and leaders to be His avengers, whom will carry out His wrath on our behalf against those who do evil to us (Romans 12:17-21).

Our job is to live peaceably with everyone so we may share the Gospel with them and fulfill the Great Commission. If someone does evil towards us, we are not to retaliate, we are to allow God to avenge us and punish them through the righteous rulers who we elect.

This is why it is important for us to be involved with politics and elect righteous rulers. We elect righteous rulers so they govern according to God's righteous precepts, they keep us safe, we live in peace and the blessings of God will overflow our nation which will allow Christians to focus on fulfilling the Great commission.

As the Gospel transforms our hearts, we will transform our culture and will transform our nation.

If we fail to engage in politics, then wicked rulers will arise and lead our country into deeper levels of darkness and sin, which will degrade our nation and bring forth the fruit of corruption and persecution.

This is exactly what happened to the Chinese Christians under the communist leader Mao Tse Tung, the German's under the socialist leader Adolf Hitler and the many other God hating marxist, socialist and communist leaders which have risen and persecuted the Church and killed untold millions in the 20th century.

Proverbs 29:2 When the righteous are in authority, the people rejoice: but when the wicked beareth rule, the people mourn.

We must heed the wisdom on these verses. We must stop believing the lie that those who hate God have told us. They will say anything to keep us out of the political arena because they love their sin and they hate righteousness. It is time for us to put the righteous in authority so that our mourning will turn to rejoicing!

The governmental systems of this world is not how God ultimately governs. This is a way of holding back the flood gates of wickedness until the Church transforms the nations through the fulfillment of the Great Commission unto the coming of Christ.

CHAPTER 9

WHAT IS GOD'S PLAN?

Let us review, we have seen that truth contradicts popular end times teaching. We have answered the question, who's left behind, the righteous or the wicked? We have discovered that unlike what the "Left Behind" books teach (the righteous taken and the wicked left behind) the Bible actually teaches the opposite. The Bible clearly teaches the wicked will be taken in judgment, removed from the earth and the righteous will be left behind to inherit the earth.

We have also answered the question, who does this earth belong to God or Satan? We, once again, saw the Bible contradicts the popular teaching that the earth belongs to the devil, and reveals the earth and everything belongs to God.

We have dealt with the rapture theory. First, we examined the Scriptures the rapture preachers so often use and proved the Scriptures they use, do not refer to being removed from the earth and being taken into heaven in the rapture. These Scriptures most often are referring to the resurrection at Christ's return.

Also, we have reviewed the teachings of the early Church fathers, the creeds and confessions of the early and historic Church. They do not even mention the rapture or anything close to the concept of the rapture.

Then we reviewed the history of this teaching and identified the rapture was invented in the 1800's, then promoted by John Nelson Darby and in the early 1900's. C. I. Scofield made the rapture popular when he included Darby's notes concerning end times and the rapture in his Scofield Reference Bible (1909).

The question remains, if everything we have been taught about the end times concerning the rapture is wrong, what is God's plan?

Let's answer this question by first defining the word "PLAN"

A plan is a strategy for doing or achieving something.

God's plan is "a strategy" for achieving His original purpose. What is God's original purpose? God's original purpose was to be in a harmonious relationship with mankind on this earth, through which He reigns over His creation in His Kingdom.

We are to carry out "the God given strategy" for achieving God's original purpose. Before we review the strategy we are to carry out to achieve God's original purpose, let us first briefly examine the original purpose then we will move on to the following topics in this order:

1. God's Original Purpose

2. God's Plan For The Earth

3. God's Plan (Strategy) For HIS Church

4. The Restoration Of Dominion

5. God's Kingdom Reign Over His Creation

CHAPTER 10

GOD'S ORIGINAL PURPOSE

The Bible doesn't say that God merely has love, it states God is love.

1 John 4:8 He that loveth not knoweth not God; for God is love.

What would it be like, to be the very embodiment of love, and have no one to love? This was God's purpose. God being the very embodiment of love, wanted children to pour Himself into and love. God wanted a family. So God created the earth and put mankind on the earth and this gave Him great pleasure.

Revelation 4:11 Thou art worthy, O Lord, to receive glory and honour and power: for thou hast created all things, and for thy pleasure they are and were created.

This is amazing. Revelation says for God's great pleasure all things were created. This brought God great pleasure to have children in His image that He may have a love relationship with, and He created this earth for that purpose.

This love relationship God wanted was to be one of free will. God did not want to create humans that were like robots who were programmed to love Him. God wanted people who would choose to love Him from their own hearts. Therefore, He created mankind with a free will and with the capacity to choose or reject Him.

God is omniscient, meaning God knows all things (1 John 3:20) and knows what will take place beforehand.

Isaiah 46:9-10 Remember the former things of old: for I am God, and there is none else; I am God, and there is none like me, (10) Declaring the end from the beginning, and from ancient times the things that are not yet done, saying, My counsel shall stand, and I will do all my pleasure:

God being omniscient, knew if He created the first human beings (Adam and Eve) with free will and gave them a choice between obedience (not eating of the forbidden tree) or rebellion (eating of the forbidden tree), they would choose to rebel (Gen 2:16-17, 3:1-7) and in choosing rebellion, they would bring forth sin into the world.

Isaiah 59:2 tells us that sin separates us from God. This is a very important point. Because God is Love, He created mankind to have a harmonious relationship with Him. However, the sin that Adam and Eve would bring into the world, would separate mankind from God and therefore undermine the whole purpose for God creating the earth and placing man therein.

Therefore, God in His foreknowledge, before He created heaven or earth, set forth a plan to remove sin and undo the separation that sin would produce. What plan is this? The plan is called the Lamb slain from the foundation of the world.

Revelation 13:8 And all that dwell upon the earth shall worship him, whose names are not written in the book of life of the Lamb slain from the foundation of the world.

This verse describes Jesus as the Lamb slain from the foundation of the world. Peter gives us more detail concerning this truth.

1 Peter 1:18-21 Forasmuch as ye know that ye were not redeemed with corruptible things, as silver and gold, from your vain conversation received by tradition from your fathers; (19) But with the precious blood of Christ, as of a lamb without blemish and without spot: (20) Who verily was foreordained before the foundation of the world, but was manifest in these last times for you, (21) Who by him do believe in God, that raised him up from the dead, and gave him glory; that your faith and hope might be in God.

Peter tells us Christ was foreordained before the foundation of the world to be the sacrifice for sin, and all who believe in Him should receive redemption, the forgiveness of sin (Eph. 1:7, Col. 1:14).

Before Adam and Eve even had a chance to sin and rebel, God in His foreknowledge, created a plan to undo and remove the sin that Adam would unleash and as a result separate man from God (Isaiah 59:2).

Hebrews 9:26 For then must he often have suffered since the foundation of the world: but now once in the end of the world hath he appeared to put away sin by the sacrifice of himself.

Peter said that Jesus was "foreordained before the foundation of the world, but was manifest in these last times for you" and the writer of Hebrews said when Christ was manifested in these last times, that "he appeared to put away sin by the sacrifice of himself."

Christ came into this world to remove the sin of Adam that separated man from God, so all those who hear the Gospel and believe in Christ, can receive forgiveness of sin and come back into harmonious relationship with the Father.

CHAPTER 11

GOD'S PLAN FOR THIS EARTH

In the creation account we see that God created the earth for mankind. God first lays the oceans, the lands, the herbs, the trees, the fruits, the vegetables, the sun, the moon, the fish, the birds and the land animals. Only after the conditions were perfect for mankind did God create man and placed them on the earth. After God placed mankind in the garden, He put everything under man's dominion and gave them their most important assignment to fill the earth with children.

Genesis 1:26-28 And God said, Let us make man in our image, after our likeness: and let them have dominion over the fish of the sea, and over the fowl of the air, and over the cattle, and over all the earth, and over every creeping thing that creepeth upon the earth. (27) So God created man in his own image, in the image of God created he him; male and female created he them. (28) And God blessed them, and God said unto them, Be fruitful, and multiply, and fill the earth, and subdue it: and have dominion over the fish of the sea, and over the fowl of the air, and over every living thing that moveth upon the earth.

In verse 26, after God created Adam and Eve in His image, He gave them dominion over the earth and all that is in it. This dominion was given to them so that they could fulfill their God given assignment.

After receiving dominion, God told them to be fruitful, multiply

115

and fill the earth. When God told them to be fruitful, He was saying reproduce children. Multiply means to reproduce "the same thing" in large numbers. Therefore, when He told them to multiply, He was saying multiply the image I created you in (God's image) in your children. God wanted His image, the image that Adam and Eve were created in, to be multiplied through their children and fill the earth.

Being fruitful, multiplying and filling the earth was their most important assignment. In other words, what God said to them was, "I want a big family so therefore fill the whole earth with children (be fruitful) who are in my image (and multiply)."

Adam and Eve failed to carry out their assignment to be fruitful, multiply and fill the earth. Instead of filling the earth with children in the image of God, they fell into sin and filled the earth with sinful humanity. They failed because they did not use their God given dominion (Genesis 1:28) to exert authority when tempted by the serpent (Genesis 3:1-7). When the serpent tempted them, they should have used their authority to take the serpent by the neck and cast out of the garden, but they didn't. As a result, they fell into sin and sin separated man from God.

Some think because of this, God is going to remove us from this earth and take us to live in heaven forever and ever. Actually, heaven is not the ultimate home for Saints but rather, heaven is the dwelling place of God and the current home of all the Christians who have died.

2 Corinthians 5:8 We are confident, I say, and willing rather to be absent from the body, and to be present with the Lord.

Philippians 1:21-25 For to me to live is Christ, and to die is gain. (22) But if I live in the flesh, this is the fruit of my labor. Yet I do not know what I shall choose. (23) For I am pressed together by the two: having a desire to depart and to be with Christ, which is far better. (24) But to remain in the flesh is more needful for you. (25) And having this confidence, I know that I shall remain and continue with you all, for your advancement and joy of faith…

In 2 Corinthians 5:8 Paul states if we are absent from the body (through death) their spirit is present with the Lord. Likewise, in Philippians 1:21-25 Paul writes if he departs through death, that he would be with the Lord. So Paul is very clear about the matter. When a Christian dies, their body lays at rest in the ground and their spirit goes to be with Jesus in heaven.

But heaven is not our ultimate home. As we have seen, the Bible does not teach that Jesus is coming to get us and take us to heaven, no instead, the Bible teaches us when Jesus comes back to this earth He is bringing all the Christians who have passed away, and who are now in heaven back with him, and we will be caught up with them in resurrection power, here in this lower atmosphere i.e. this earth.

1 Thessalonians 4:13-14 (13) But I would not have you to be ignorant, brethren, concerning them which are asleep, that ye sorrow not, even as others which have no hope. (14) For if we believe that Jesus died and rose again, even so them also which sleep in Jesus will God bring with him.

At the end of verse 14 we read Jesus is bringing those who are in heaven back to earth with Him. We must understand why Jesus is bringing the Christians in heaven back to this earth with Him. This is because God is not a loser, His original plan for the earth has not changed. After Adam fell into sin, God did not lose this earth to Satan. This earth, as we have proved, has never belonged to Satan and has always belonged to God. Let us look at what Isaiah says about this earth.

Isaiah 45:17-18 But Israel shall be saved in the LORD with an everlasting salvation: ye shall not be ashamed nor confounded world without end. (18) For thus saith the LORD that created the heavens; God himself that formed the earth and made it; he hath established it, he created it not in vain, he formed it to be inhabited: I am the LORD; and there is none else.

In verse 17, Isaiah writes Israel shall be saved with everlasting salvation. That is salvation that goes on forever and ever. At the end of the verse he says you shall not be ashamed nor confounded "world without end." World without end simply means there is no end to time which means eternity.

In the next verse, right after he sets the context of salvation and time, with "forever and ever" and "world without end" Isaiah says that God formed the earth and established it. He continues and states God didn't create the earth in vain (empty of purpose, void of purpose or without purpose) but He formed it with the purpose of being inhabited.

God's message through Isaiah is "despite the sin that came into this world through Adam, I have made available through Christ everlasting salvation and my original purpose for creating the earth is not in vain (empty of purpose, void of purpose or without purpose), because I formed the earth to be inhabited by mankind, so I can have a glorious and harmonious love relationship with them."

God is saying His plan for the earth has not changed but will be fulfilled. The earth will be the location on which God fulfills His ultimate desire to have children that He can love while being loved by them. It is all about a love relationship with God here on the earth.

Some reading this might be asking the question "I thought God was going to destroy this earth with fire?" This is true but the context in which the Bible teaches is a little different than we have been taught.

Revelation 21 is talking about the new heavens and earth. And concerning the new heavens and earth John writes a very important detail. Let us start in verse 1 then we will review verse 5.

Revelation 21:1 And I saw a new heaven and a new earth: for the first heaven and the first earth were passed away; and there was no more sea.

John says he saw a new heaven and a new earth, for the first heaven and the first earth were passed away. Verse 5 sets the context which informs us about how the new heaven and earth comes to being and how the old heaven and earth passes away.

Revelation 21:5 And he that sat upon the throne said, Behold, I make all things new. And he said unto me, Write: for these words are true and faithful.

God said of the new heavens and earth "Behold, I make all things new." Notice He did not say "I make all new things" no He said "I make all things new." In other words, He is not going to obliterate this earth and make a completely new one, instead the impurities will be burnt out of it by the refiner's fire of His judgment when He comes back.

Let us investigate Peter's writings on this subject.

2 Peter 2:1-5 But there were false prophets also among the people, even as there shall be false teachers among you, who privily shall bring in damnable heresies, even denying the Lord that bought them, and bring upon themselves swift destruction. (2) And many shall follow their pernicious ways; by reason of whom the way of truth shall be evil spoken of. (3) And through covetousness shall they with feigned words make merchandise of you: whose judgment now of a long time lingereth not, and their damnation slumbereth not. (4) For if God spared not the angels that sinned, but cast them down to hell, and delivered them into chains of darkness, to be reserved unto judgment; (5) And spared not the old world, but saved Noah the eighth person, a preacher of righteousness, bringing in the flood upon the world of the ungodly;

In verses 1 through 4 Peter tells of the wicked and the coming judgment that awaits them. Then in verse 5 Peter gives the example of Noah saying God did not spare the old world but saved Noah while He brought judgment on the wicked.

From here we notice three things. 1) God did not spare the old world. In other words, He judged it. 2) God saved Noah. 3) God judged and destroyed the wicked. These three things are the pattern Peter is giving us for the coming judgment and renewal of the earth.

This is the same pattern that Jesus gave us in Matthew 24:36-42 and Luke 17:27. Remember, as it was in the days of Noah, so shall it be in the coming of the Son of man. The wicked was eating and drinking, marrying and given in marriage, and the wicked did not know anything until the flood came and took them away (or destroyed them as the Luke account articulates).

The judgment that came in Noah's day destroyed the wicked and their works, taking them away, while Noah was saved and left behind. Noah and the righteous inherited the earth (the same earth) while the wicked and their works were removed in judgment. Peter elaborates on this in the next chapter.

2 Peter 3:7-13 But the heavens and the earth, which are now, by the same word are kept in store, reserved unto fire against the day of judgment and perdition of ungodly men. (8) But, beloved, be not ignorant of this one thing, that one day is with the Lord as a thousand years, and a thousand years as one day. (9) The Lord is not slack concerning his promise, as some men count slackness; but is longsuffering to us-ward, not willing that any should perish, but that all should come to repentance. (10) But the day of the Lord will come as a thief in the night; in the which the heavens shall pass away with a great noise, and the elements shall melt with fervent heat, the earth also and the works that are therein shall be burned up. (11) Seeing then that all these things shall be dissolved, what manner of persons ought ye to be in all holy conversation and godliness, (12) Looking for and hasting unto the coming of the day of God, wherein the heavens being on fire shall be dissolved, and the elements shall melt with fervent heat? (13) Nevertheless we, according to his promise, look for new heavens and a new earth, wherein dwelleth righteousness.

Verse 7 says that the heavens and the earth which are now, are kept in store, reserved unto fire against the Day of Judgment and perdition of ungodly men. Verse 10 through 12 says the heavens being on fire will dissolve, the elements will melt with fervent heat, the earth and its works will be burnt up, then verse 13 says nevertheless, we look for a new heaven and earth wherein dwells righteousness.

We see this same idea in 1 Corinthians as Paul tells us that our works will be judged by fire.

1 Corinthians 3:10-15 According to the grace of God which is given unto me, as a wise masterbuilder, I have laid the foundation, and another buildeth thereon. But let every man take heed how he buildeth thereupon. (11) For other foundation can no man lay than that is laid, which is Jesus Christ. (12) Now if any man build upon this foundation gold, silver, precious stones, wood, hay, stubble; (13) Every man's work shall be made manifest: for the day shall declare it, because it shall be revealed by fire; and the fire shall try every man's work of what sort it is. (14) If any man's work abide which he hath built thereupon, he shall receive a reward. (15) If any man's work shall be burned, he shall suffer loss: but he himself shall be saved; yet so as by fire.

When Christ comes back, the wicked will be judged, the heavens and earth will be purged with the refiner's fire of His judgment (1 Peter 3:10, 1 Corinthians 3:15), then will appear in its full the new heaven and earth on which the resurrected Saints will dwell with God forever. Remember, God is not making new things, He's making all things new (Revelation 21:1-5).

God created this earth for His family and nowhere in the Bible does He change His plan. The earth still belongs to Him, and He still plans to fill it with His children for the purpose of relationship.

CHAPTER 12

GOD'S PLAN FOR HIS CHURCH

God created this earth and placed mankind on the earth for the purpose of having a relationship. Adam sinned and his sin separated man from God. God knew this was going to happen, so He foreordained Jesus from before the foundations of the world, to remove sin by the sacrifice of Himself (Hebrews 9:26). And now everyone who hears the Gospel and receives forgiveness of sins through faith in Jesus Christ, is restored to unbroken relationship and fellowship with God.

God's original purpose of having a family that fills the earth, is restored through the redemptive work of Jesus Christ. What Adam and Eve failed to do (be fruitful, multiply and fill the earth), God has commanded His Church to complete. When Jesus rose from the dead, He picked up the baton that Adam dropped and passed that baton to the Church. Now, it is the mission of Believers everywhere to be fruitful, multiply and fill the earth.

No, I am not saying we need to start having babies. What I am saying is we have the same mandate, as revealed by the pattern given to Adam and Eve. It is the same mission to accomplish, but we achieve this in a different way.

Matthew 28:19-20 Go ye therefore, and make disciples of all nations, baptizing them in the name of the Father, and of the Son, and of the Holy Ghost: (20) Teaching them to observe all things whatsoever I have commanded you: and, lo, I am with you always, even unto the end of the world. Amen.

Jesus is giving us the Great Commission. This is God's plan for the Church. He is giving us our marching orders which is to make disciples of all nations.

He did not say do your best to share the Gospel with a few people in each nation. No the mandate is clear, we are to make disciples of ALL NATIONS. This is the original purpose of God, that we are called to fulfill. We "be fruitful, multiply and fill the earth" with God's children, through saving the lost and making disciples of every nation.

Most people see the Great Commission as our attempt to save a few sinners before Jesus comes back. Although the Great Commission involves saving sinners through the preaching of the Gospel, there is much more. This is God's method to achieve His original desire to have a family that fills the earth.

Salvation is but the starting point. This is the door through which one enters into a relationship with God through Jesus Christ. As a result, they are His children and God is their Father. This new relationship with the Father must grow until their whole life reflects Him and this is where discipleship comes in.

The Great Commission is given to us in two places, Mark 16:15-20 and Matthew 28:18-20. In Mark 16:15-20 Jesus emphasizes going into all the world and saving the lost. In Matthew 28:18-20 He emphasizes going into all the world and making disciples of all nations.

I often hear Christians debate whether the focus should be on saving the lost or making disciples. I have heard very passionate cases from both sides. I personally think the debates are needless because we are not to choose between either. The reason for this is saving the lost and making disciples are two sides of the same coin. The Great Commission is both. You cannot make a disciple unless they first are saved. Another way of saying this is, you cannot clean a fish unless you first catch the fish.

We must go into all the world and save the lost, then make them into disciples. Two points concerning this:

1) Unless a person is first saved and converted in their heart, they will never submit to discipleship and reflect the relationship with the Father in their life.

2) A person that is saved must be brought into the process of discipleship, for the Great Commission is to save the lost and make disciples.

If we are only offering salvation to the lost, our efforts are incomplete. This would be like a married couple having a child but not committing to feeding, nurturing, and training the child as they grow, in order to equip and prepare them for life. We must not only be committed to save them, but also to feed, nurture, and train them so they can grow into mature sons and daughters of God.

Salvation redeems man from the sin Adam brought them into while he (Adam) was in the Garden, and makes them (the new Christian) into children of God. Discipleship brings them out of the lifestyle that Adam's sin produced in their life, into a new holy way of living, which reflects the character and nature of God our Father.

When a person is saved they literally become a new person on the inside.

2 Corinthians 5:17 Therefore if any man be in Christ, he is a new creature: old things are passed away; behold, all things are become new.

Paul tells us because you came to Christ, you became a new person. He says the "old things" meaning your sin and your old sinful life passed away i.e. died.

God did this by removing your old sinful heart and giving you a new heart, a new nature and placing His Holy Spirit on the inside of you. By doing this God empowers you to live this new life as God's child.

Ezekiel 36:26 A new heart also will I give you, and a new spirit will I put within you: and I will take away the stony heart out of your flesh, and I will give you an heart of flesh.

God said when you are saved, I am going to change you on the inside. As you learn of this change and learn of God's ways (being discipled) you will start to reflect that change on the outside, and it will be seen in every part of your life. People will know that God is your Father and you are His child.

After the heart is changed, any area and/or arena of life the disciple may find them-self in, whether it be business, government, media, arts and entertainment, education, the family and/or religion, will conform to the culture of God and become the mission field of that Believer. God not only wants the individual, but He wants every aspect of their life.

Furthermore, God not only wants the individual and every aspect of their life, but He wants all people, from every nation, every tribe and every tongue to be a part of His family and reflect His Glory in their lives. He also wants the whole earth to come under His possession. This is the motive of Jesus and the reason He gave us the Great Commission.

Psalms 2:7-8 I will declare the decree: the LORD hath said unto me, Thou art my Son; this day have I begotten thee. (8) Ask of me, and I shall give thee the heathen for thine inheritance, and the uttermost parts of the earth for thy possession.

Psalms 2:7-8 is a prophecy of the resurrected Christ. The Father says to Jesus "Thou art my Son; this day have I begotten thee." This is what Paul was quoting in Acts 13.

Acts 13:33 God hath fulfilled the same unto us their children, in that he hath raised up Jesus again; as it is also written in the second psalm, Thou art my Son, this day have I begotten thee.

The second Psalm is clearly talking about the resurrected Christ. Now, look in Psalms 2:8 and take note of the reward that God the Father promises the resurrected Christ, if He just asks for it.

Psalms 2:8 Ask of me, and I shall give thee the heathen for thine inheritance, and the uttermost parts of the earth for thy possession.

Father God told Jesus, ask of me and I will give you the "heathen" for your inheritance. The Hebrew word for "heathen" is "goy" and means nations. God said ask of me and I will give you the NATIONS for your inheritance and the uttermost parts of the EARTH for thy possession.

Why would Father God make the promise to give the resurrected Jesus these things if He just asked for them? Because Jesus came in order to restore the original purpose of God, for a love relationship with His creation, by removing the sin that separated them.

Jesus, through His death and resurrection, made the way available for those who are separated from God by their sin, to receive forgiveness and be restored to a relationship with the Father. Now that restoration is made, people must find out about it. This is the reason for the Great Commission.

When the risen Christ says to the Father, give me the nations for my inheritance and the ends of the earth for my possession, the risen Christ then turns around and gives the Great Commission to His disciples.

He tells them to "go into all the world and make disciples of all nations". In other words, what Jesus is saying to them is "the Father promised me the nations for my inheritance and the uttermost parts of the earth for my possession, so go into all the world and get what belongs to me. I want my inheritance and I want to take possession of the earth."

Christ is sending us into all the earth to tell the nations that sin has been removed and there is now a door open through Christ, by which they can enter into a relationship with the Father.

As we go forth and herald this wonderful message, we will be fruitful, multiply and fill the earth with disciples, Christ then, will begin to take dominion. All nations will come to Him and bow their knee, not in un-willful submission, but in thankfulness, adoration and praise.

Christ, who at that time has the nations for His inheritance and ends of the earth for His possessions, will come back, consummate all things, hand it all over to the Father (1 Corinthians 15:24), that He may have a family that fills the earth just like He desires. God's original intent for creation is finally fulfilled.

CHAPTER 13

THE RESTORATION OF DOMINION

Our mission is to reproduce and multiply and fill the earth with God's children (Christians). We accomplish this by saving the lost and making disciples of all nations. God does not tell us to fulfill His plan with our own strength. As a matter of fact, fulfilling the plan of God by human strength or intellect is impossible.

God not only restored the Genesis mandate to reproduce, multiply and fill the earth, but He also restored the dominion and authority to accomplish our mission. We must learn from the mistake of Adam and Eve, who, when tested by the serpent failed to use their dominion. We, however, must not fail to use our Kingdom dominion to complete our mission.

Before Jesus died and rose again, Satan had authority over all mankind because all mankind was bound by sin. But Jesus came to destroy the works of the devil and put an end to Satan's reign over man.

1 John 3:8 He that committeth sin is of the devil; for the devil sinneth from the beginning. For this purpose the Son of God was manifested, that he might destroy the works of the devil.

Jesus came with the express purpose to destroy the works of the devil. That includes Satan's efforts to destroy the plan of God of having an earth filled with children, by causing Adam and Eve to abort the mission through their rebellion.

Jesus was focused on stripping Satan of his authority and redeeming mankind from their sin. Just as the serpent took dominion over man in a garden, Jesus starts the process to take dominion back from Satan in a garden.

In the Garden of Gethsemane, Jesus sweat great drops of blood, as He prayed in agony concerning the cross and the work He would do to redeem mankind (Luke 22:39-46). A garden is where His redemptive act would begin, where He was buried, where He rose again and where Mary mistook Him for the gardener (John 19:40-42, 20:15).

What Mary was soon to find out was, it was Jesus and He was in fact the gardener (the Last Adam, 1 Cor. 15:45) who, through the cross kicked the serpent out of the garden as He rose again victorious. Let us look at the cross and see how it happened.

John 12:31-33 Now is the judgment of this world: now shall the prince of this world be cast out. (32) And I, if I be lifted up from the earth, will draw all men unto me. (33) This he said, signifying what death he should die.

In John 12:31 Jesus says now, the prince of this world is going to be judged and cast out. Jesus is saying Satan's time of reigning over man, by keeping them trapped in sin, has come to an end. It is now time to dethrone him and cast him out.

The next two verses make it very clear that Jesus is speaking of His death on the cross. In verse 32 Jesus says if "I be lifted up", speaking of being lifted up on the cross. Verse 33 says "this He said signifying what kind of death He should die."

Therefore, Satan being cast out is the result of the work of Christ on the cross. Why did the work of the cross strip Satan of his authority over mankind? Because sin gave Satan power over man. As Jesus was nailed to the cross, His precious blood was being spilled and He was purchasing the forgiveness of sin for man (Ephesians 1:7).

Through His blood, Christ made a way for mankind to break free from the shackles of sin, and thus escaping the dictatorship of Satan. No longer could Satan hold sway over any person who chose to believe the Gospel and submit to the Lordship of Christ. Colossians chapter 2 expounds on this point.

Colossians 2:14-15 Blotting out the handwriting of ordinances that was against us, which was contrary to us, and took it out of the way, nailing it to his cross; (15) And having spoiled principalities and powers, he made a shew of them openly, triumphing over them in it.

This is saying, that all the sin that Satan could accuse you of was nailed to Christ's cross. The blood of Christ truly forgives all sin and sets man free from Satan's power. That is why, because of the blood, Jesus spoiled principalities and powers, He made a show of them openly, triumphing over them in it.

Spoiled means to disarm and strip. Through the cross Jesus disarmed and stripped Satan of His authority. He made an open show and triumphed over Satan victoriously. Then Jesus rose again with all authority, all power and all dominion.

Ephesians 1:19-23 And what is the exceeding greatness of his power to us-ward who believe, according to the working of his mighty power, (20) Which he wrought in Christ, when he raised him from the dead, and set him at his own right hand in the heavenly places, (21) Far above all principality, and power, and might, and dominion, and every name that is named, not only in this world, but also in that which is to come: (22) And hath put all things under his feet, and gave him to be the head over all things to the Church, (23) Which is his body, the fulness of him that filleth all in all.

In verse 19, Paul is praying the Church in Ephesus would receive a revelation of the exceeding greatness of his power that works in them. This, as Paul clarifies, is resurrection power. He explains in the following verses, this is the very same power that God worked in Christ when He raised Him from the dead and sat Him at His own right hand.

In verse 21, Paul gives details about what this resurrection power did for Christ when He was raised. Paul says this resurrection raised Christ far above all principality, and power, and might, and dominion, and every name that is named, not only in this world, but also in that which is to come. In verse 22-23, Paul says that this power put all things under Christ's feet and made Him to be head over the Church which is His body.

This means when Christ was raised from the dead He became the supreme power in heaven and earth. He was made head of the Church which is His body. He is the head and we are the body, which means through our union with Him, we share in this resurrection power (Ephesians 2:5-6). This is exactly why Paul was praying the Church in Ephesus would receive a revelation of the exceeding greatness of His power (Supreme Resurrection Power) that works in them.

Matthew 28:18-20 And Jesus came and spake unto them, saying, All authority is given unto me in heaven and in earth. (19) Go ye therefore, and make disciples of all nations, baptizing them in the name of the Father, and of the Son, and of the Holy Ghost: (20) Teaching them to observe all things whatsoever I have commanded you: and, lo, I am with you always, even unto the end of the world. Amen.

Christ went to the cross and made redemption for sin and thus stripping Satan of his authority. He then rose from the dead with supreme authority over all principality, power, and might, and dominion and with everything placed under His feet.

The risen Christ, calls a meeting with His disciples (Matthew 28:16) and at this meeting, Jesus declares unto them all authority has been given to Him in heaven and earth. Then He commissioned them with that authority to make disciples of all nations.

Adam lost dominion to the serpent in the Garden but Jesus took it back through the cross. Satan has no power to stop the Church from taking the Gospel into all the earth and making disciples of all nations. We must use our dominion and fulfill our mission.

PONCE LEON

CHAPTER 14

GOD'S KINGDOM REIGN OVER HIS CREATION

In the previous chapter we learned Jesus took back the dominion that Adam lost and gave it to His Church to fulfill the Great Commission. In Matthew 28:18 the resurrected Christ declared all authority has been given to me in heaven and earth, then He commissioned us with that authority to save the lost and make disciples of all nations. We have the authority of King Jesus to fulfill our mission.

In this chapter we will learn not only have we been given back the dominion that Adam lost which is the "Authority of the King", but also, we have been given the "Power of His Kingdom."

The Authority of the King is like a police officer's badge, and the power of the Kingdom, is like the police officers gun. We have the authority and power to make disciples of all nations!

We are not merely Christians who are trying to share the Gospel with a few lost people, no, we are Kings and Priests of God (2 Peter 2:9, Rev. 1:6) and we have been empowered to reign on the earth (Rev. 5:10). We go forth as Kings and Priests and share the Gospel in the authority of the King and the power of

His Kingdom.

This authority and power that Christ gives us to accomplish the Great Commission is authority and power that comes from the throne. When Jesus rose from the dead He was seated at the right hand of the Father on His throne and He empowered us to go forth in this Kingdom dominion.

The resurrection marks the beginning of His Kingdom. Of this event Daniel writes the following.

Daniel 7:13-14 I was watching in the night visions, And behold, One like the Son of Man, Coming with the clouds of heaven! He came to the Ancient of Days, and they brought Him near before Him. (14) Then to Him was given dominion and glory and a kingdom, that all peoples, nations, and languages should serve Him. His dominion is an everlasting dominion, which shall not pass away, And His kingdom the one which shall not be destroyed.

When Christ (the Son of Man) rose in power, He went before the Father (the Ancient of Days) and He was given dominion, glory and a Kingdom that all peoples, nations and languages should serve Him.

This is saying the dominion and the Kingdom (Kingdom Dominion) was given to Him for the purpose of making disciples of all nations. This is the Authority that He gave to us when He commissioned us with the Great Commission.

Also, in Acts chapter 2 on the day of Pentecost, we read this very same thing. When Christ was raised from the dead, He was seated on the throne (He received a Kingdom) from which He poured out the Holy Spirit.

Acts 2:29-35 Men and brethren, let me freely speak unto you of the patriarch David, that he is both dead and buried, and his tomb is with us unto this day. (30) Therefore being a prophet, and knowing that God had sworn with an oath to him, that of the fruit of his loins, according to the flesh, he would raise up Christ to sit on his throne; (31) He foreseeing this, spoke of the resurrection of Christ, that his soul was not left in hell, neither his flesh did see corruption. (32) This Jesus hath God raised up, whereof we all are witnesses. (33) Therefore being by the right hand of God exalted, and having received of the Father the promise of the Holy Ghost, he hath shed forth this, which ye now see and hear. (34) For David is not ascended into the heavens: but he saith himself, The LORD said unto my Lord, Sit thou on my right hand, (35) Until I make thy foes thy footstool.

In verse 30 Peter said David being a prophet, knew that God would fulfill the oath to him by raising Christ up to sit on his throne. The oath that is being referred to here, was the oath that God made to David to raise up his seed to inherit his throne and God would establish that Kingdom forever (Ps. 132:11, 2Sam. 7:12, Luke 1:32). Then in the next verse it says that he foreseeing this, spoke of the resurrection of Christ. In other words, Christ was raised up and given the throne of David on which He reigns until He makes all the enemies of God His footstool (Acts 2:29-35).

This happened in the resurrection. Christ is now seated in heaven, ruling through His Church until all enemies are made His footstool. How does Christ make all enemies His footstool? He does this through the Great Commission. As we are fruitful, multiply and fill the earth with God's children, by saving the lost and making disciples of all nations, everyone and everything will ultimately come under the dominion of Christ.

In order for the Church to fulfill this task, we are empowered by the Authority of the King (Matt. 28:18-20, Mark 16:15-20) and the power of the Kingdom (Acts 1:5, 8, Acts 2:33). Let us take a look.

In verse 32-33 Peter proclaims this Jesus, God raised up and exalted Him to the right hand of God, to sit on the throne from where He poured out the Holy Spirit.

The question we must ask is why did Christ pour out the Holy Spirit? We find the answer in the previous chapter.

Acts 1:5-8 For John truly baptized with water; but ye shall be baptized with the Holy Ghost not many days hence. (6) When they therefore were come together, they asked of him, saying, Lord, will thou at this time restore again the kingdom to Israel? (7) And he said unto them, It is not for you to know the times or the seasons, which the Father hath put in his own power. (8) But ye shall receive power, after that the Holy Ghost is come upon you: and ye shall be witnesses unto me both in Jerusalem, and in all Judaea, and in Samaria, and unto the uttermost part of the earth.

In verse 5 Jesus tells His disciples they are going to be baptized by the Spirit not many days from then. Then the disciples responded by asking Jesus if the Kingdom was going to be restored. Many people say that Jesus never answers their question. They say by Jesus replying "it isn't for them to know the times or seasons which the Father has put in His own power", He was telling the disciples it was none of their business.

Although this is true that Jesus replied this way, it is not true that Jesus did not answer them. After He told them in verse 7, it is not for them to know the times or seasons, Jesus starts out in verse 8 by saying "but." In other words He is saying "it is not for you to know the times or seasons 'but' I will tell you." Then Jesus tells them. He answers them by saying you shall receive power (the Kingdom) after the Holy Spirit has come upon you.

Remember, the disciples asked about the coming of the Kingdom (verse 6) after Jesus told them they would be baptized in the Holy Spirit (verse 5). Why would the disciples ask about the Kingdom after being told they would be baptized by the Holy Spirit?

The answer is, because of their time with Christ, they learned to associate the coming of the Kingdom of God with the coming of the Holy Spirit. Note the following verse:

Matthew 12:28 But if I cast out demons by the Spirit of God, then the kingdom of God has come to you.

In Matthew, Jesus linked the work of the Holy Spirit with the coming of God's Kingdom.

When the disciples heard Jesus tell them they were going to be baptized with the Holy Spirit, they associated the coming of the Holy Spirit with the coming of the Kingdom and promptly asked Jesus; which Jesus replied that it is not for them to know the times or seasons, but (but here's the answer), you shall receive power (receive the Kingdom), when the Holy Spirit comes upon you.

As Paul says in 1 Corinthians 4:20 "For the kingdom of God is not in word, but in power." And when the Holy Spirit came upon them, He came in power (with the Kingdom).

Romans 14:17 also bears witness to what was taking place in the book of Acts chapter 2, on the day of Pentecost, when the Holy Spirit was poured out on the Church.

Romans 14:17 For the kingdom of God is not meat and drink; but righteousness, and peace, and joy in the Holy Ghost.

In this verse Paul gives us the location of the Kingdom which is "in" the Holy Ghost. The Holy Ghost was poured out on the Church on the day of Pentecost. So, in Acts chapter 1 when Jesus told the disciples they were going to be baptized by the Holy Spirit, and they would receive power, He was informing them that the Kingdom of God was coming in power and they were to be the recipients.

Then in Acts chapter 2, we witness the disciples being baptized with the Holy Spirit and speak in tongues, which caused a frenzy when the people from every region and country heard the Gospel in their own language (Act 2:1-12).

Peter then told the people what they were witnessing was the outpouring of the Holy Spirit (the invasion of the Kingdom) as a result of Jesus being raised to the throne and receiving the Kingdom (Daniel 7:13-14, Acts 2:29-35).

As the Holy Spirit was poured out on the Church, the Kingdom came in power for the purpose of making disciples of every nation as stated in Daniel 7:13-14 and Acts 1:8. Let us review these 2 verses in order to reemphasize and establish this point.

Daniel 7:13-14 I was watching in the night visions, And behold, One like the Son of Man, Coming with the clouds of heaven!

He came to the Ancient of Days, and they brought Him near before Him. (14) Then to Him was given dominion and glory and a kingdom, that all peoples, nations, and languages should serve Him. His dominion is an everlasting dominion, which shall not pass away, And His kingdom the one which shall not be destroyed.

After the resurrection, Jesus (the Son of Man), came before the Father (the Ancient of Days) in order to receive dominion and glory and a Kingdom. Notice for what purpose… "that all peoples, nations, and languages should serve Him." Now Acts Chapter 1.

Acts 1:8 But ye shall receive power, after that the Holy Ghost is come upon you: and ye shall be witnesses unto me both in Jerusalem, and in all Judaea, and in Samaria, and unto the uttermost part of the earth.

Jesus said you shall receive power after the Holy Ghost has come upon you. Again, notice for what purpose… "and ye shall be witnesses unto me both in Jerusalem, and in all Judaea, and in Samaria, and unto the uttermost part of the earth."

Just like God gave Adam dominion to fulfill his mandate to be fruitful, multiply and fill the earth with God's children, He gives us dominion to do the same through the Great Commission.

As we go forth and save the lost and make disciples, the same dominion we use to fulfill our mission, then begins to rule in the lives of all those that we bring to Christ and disciple.

When a person is not saved, they are lost and still under the sway of Satan (2 Cor. 4:4), trapped in darkness and that darkness reigns in their hearts (Eph. 4:17-18) and manifests itself in various levels of corrupt sinful lifestyles. When a person gets born again, they become brand new on the inside and the Holy Spirit moves into them (Ezekiel 36:26, 1 Cor. 3:16). When this happens two things take place: 1) they are delivered from the bondage of darkness and are translated into the Kingdom of God. 2) God sets up His Kingdom on the inside of them.

Colossians 1:13 Who hath delivered us from the power of darkness, and hath translated us into the kingdom of his dear Son:

When a person gives their life to Christ, they are instantly delivered from the power of darkness that once had them bound, and are immediately translated into the Kingdom of God.

Their sinful heart is removed and the Holy Spirit takes residence on the inside of them.

Romans 14:17 For the kingdom of God is not meat and drink; but righteousness, and peace, and joy in the Holy Ghost.

The Kingdom is located in the Holy Spirit, so when the Spirit moved into their heart, the Kingdom of God is set up on the inside of them. Now we can understand what Jesus meant when He was asked about the coming of the Kingdom in Luke 17.

Luke 17:20-21 And when he was demanded of the Pharisees, when the kingdom of God should come, he answered them and said, The kingdom of God cometh not with observation: (21) Neither shall they say, Lo here! or, lo there! for, behold, the kingdom of God is within you.

This is awesome. The Pharisees asked when the Kingdom of

God would come and Jesus tells them it does not come with observation. In others words, stop waiting to see a golden castle pop out of the sky. Neither will they say look here and look there. Why? Because you cannot see the Kingdom of God with your natural eyes. Then Jesus tells them, when the Kingdom of God comes, it will be within us.

Why does He tell them that the Kingdom of God will be within us? Because the location of the Kingdom is in the Holy Spirit, and when we are born again the Holy Spirit comes to live within us. The Holy Spirit brings God's Kingdom with Him, and sets it up in our hearts. Now God can start ruling our lives from His Kingdom from within our very hearts. Our hearts become the throne on which God rules every aspect of our lives (1 Peter 3:15).

Just like God gave Adam dominion to fulfill his calling, God has given the Church the dominion of Christ that comes from His throne (the Authority of the King and Power of His Kingdom) so we can fulfill our mission to be fruitful, multiply and fill the earth with God's children by saving the lost and making disciples of all nations.

By fulfilling the Great Commission, most everyone and most everything will ultimately come under the dominion of Christ and His Kingdom here and now.

CHAPTER 15

A CHRONOLOGY OF EVENTS

Creation –

1. God is love (1 John 4:8) and created all things for His great pleasure (Rev. 4:11) because He wanted a family that He can love and have harmonious relationship with.
2. God created Adam and Eve and gave them dominion to complete their God given assignment to be fruitful, multiply and fill the earth with children for God's family (Gen. 1:26-28).

The Fall –

1. Before Adam could be fruitful, multiply and fill the earth with children, he rebelled (Gen. 2:17, Gen. 3:1-7) against God and brought sin into this world (Rom. 5:12) which separated mankind from God (Isa. 59:2).
2. Instead of exercising his dominion and kicking the serpent out of the Garden, he lost his dominion to the serpent by becoming subject to him through sin and death (Gen. 3:1-7).
3. Mankind (sinful man) and their works came under the dominion of Satan (Luke 4:6, 2 Cor. 4:4).

4. Satan only gained dominion over fallen sinful man and their ways, not the earth. The earth and everything in it still belonged to God (Ex. 19:5, Ps. 24:1, 1 Cor. 10:26).

The Cross –

1. Jesus was manifested in this world to remove the sin that separated man from God through His death, burial and resurrection (John. 1:29, Heb. 9:28, 1 Peter 1:19-21).
2. All who repent and believe on Him receives forgiveness of sin and are restored to the family of God (John 1:12, Eph. 1:7).

The Great Commission –

1. During His death, burial and resurrection Jesus, dethroned Satan, took back dominion from him, by providing a way for man to break free from the shackles of sin through His blood, and rose again with all power, might, dominion and name, placed under His feet (John 12:31, Col. 2:14-15, Eph. 1:18-23).
2. After His resurrection, Jesus called a meeting with His disciples (Matt. 28:16) and there is where He restored the Eden mandate to be fruitful, multiply and fill the earth with God's children by saving the lost and making disciples of all nations (Matt. 18-20).
3. Just before Jesus restored the Eden mandate, He declared all authority in heaven and on earth was given to Him (Matt. 28:18). He then commissioned them with that authority which is in His name (Mark 16:17) to fulfill their mission.

Pentecost –

1. On the day of Pentecost (Acts 2) as the Holy Spirit was poured out from the throne of Christ on the Church (Acts 2:29-35) the Holy Spirit brought the Kingdom of God with power (Rom. 14:17, Acts 1:5-8).
2. At this point the Church received both the authority (Matt. 28:18) that is in His name (Mark 16:17) which is the authority of the King, but also, the power of the Kingdom (Acts 1:5-8) to fulfill the great commission.

The Fulfilling of the Great Commission –

1. As we go and save the lost and make disciples of all nations, every nation, tribe and tongue comes under the dominion of Jesus Christ and His Kingdom is increased. As the Gospel transforms their hearts, their culture will reflect it and their nations will come to predominantly honor Christ (Ps. 2:7-8, Isa. 11:9, Hab. 2:14).
2. Not all will be converted and become disciples, but the Great Commission and the Gospel will prevail in all the nations which will usher in the return of Christ (Act 2:34-35, 1 Cor. 15:23-28).

The Coming of Christ –

1. When Christ comes back this will mark the end (1 Cor. 15:24) when He will resurrect the just and the unjust (John 5:28-29, Acts 24:15). The just being raised in resurrection power and receiving their glorified bodies (John 5:28-29, 1 Cor. 15:51-57, 1 Thess. 4:13-17), the sinner will be judged and destroyed (John 5:28-29) and the old heaven and earth will be replaced by the fullness

of the new heaven and earth on which we will dwell forever with God (2 Peter 3:8-13, Rev. 21:1-5).

This represents a general outline and in no way is fully comprehensive. There are a lot of nuances that need to be articulated in order to bring a cohesive understanding to the unfolding of the historic work and flow of the Church to the consummate end.

This simple outline provides a basic chronology of events to give us a picture of what has happened and where we are headed.

CONCLUSION

We have examined the sources, so often used by those who preach the rapture. In every instance, we have found there is no evidence to support their claims of a rapture. Here is a quick recap.

1. The earth does not belong to the devil; the earth belongs to God.

2. Sinners will be removed from this earth through judgment.

3. The righteous will be left behind to inherit the new earth and dwell here forever.

4. Not one Scripture we have examined says the righteous will be physically removed from the earth and taken to heaven.

5. None of the early Church fathers taught the rapture or leaving this earth and going to heaven.

6. Likewise, none of the early Church creeds and confessions mention anything about the rapture or the Church being removed from this earth and going to heaven.

7. The rapture doctrine was in fact started in the 1800's and made popular by John Nelson Darby and C. I. Scofield.

8. God never changed His mind about His original plan for a family on this earth.

9. We were given the Great Commission to fulfill God's original plan by making disciples of all nations.

We can conclude, that the rapture, is not in any way a part of God's end time road map, which will guide us to the divine destination which Christ our Lord has died and rose again to achieve.

Therefore, if we embrace and adhere to the rapture teaching, we knowingly take an unnecessary detour, which will hinder and in many cases do damage to the overall flow and fulfillment of God's plan. A tragic example of what this misconception can lead to is seen in the Chinese Church. At the rise of communism they expected to escape the imminent persecution through the rapture, but instead of escaping, millions of Christians were tortured to death.

Consider if the Chinese Church had God's end time road map and instead of planning on escaping, they prepared for the coming persecution. Perhaps they could have saved untold millions by their preparation and the preaching of the Gospel.

Even more, if they had the correct road map, the Chinese Church could have trained up God fearing political leaders who would have become God's ministers in the Chinese government (Rom. 4:13) and prevented the communist regime from ever coming to power.

If this had been the case, they could have prevented the deaths of over 70,000,000 Chinese people and created a nation where everyone could have lived peaceably with each other; while Christians were bringing all of China and the surrounding nations under the dominion of Christ by saving the lost and making disciples of them.

I, however, give thanks to the Lord, not even persecution could stop His Church from growing. What Satan meant for harm, God has definitely brought good out of. The Chinese Church has grown exponentially under the persecution and has set such a great example for Christians all over the world. However, we shouldn't need persecution to grow, Christianity should grow because of our passionate commitment to fulfill the Great Commission.

Persecution will always be present until Christ comes back. We can prevail and overcome by saving the lost and making disciples, not primarily as a response of persecution, but as a response to the command of Jesus given in the Great Commission. If we truly call Jesus our Lord, then we will do what He says.

Luke 6:46 And why call ye me, Lord, Lord, and do not the things which I say?

Jesus gave us a clear command to save the lost and make disciples of all nations. If He truly is my Lord and your Lord, then we will lay down all, take up our cross and commit to fulfill His command.

By following and fulfilling His plan, we will ultimately arrive at the place where all nations overwhelmingly come to Christ and submit to His Lordship.

As a byproduct of the Great Commission, the earth will be filled with a family for God to enjoy. At the end, Christ will come back, Judge the sinner out of the earth, and on the new earth the resurrected Saints shall live with God forever.

So unpack your bags, embrace your mission to take dominion in the earth and make disciples of all nations!

WE ARE JUST GETTING STARTED

This book was written for 2 primary reasons. 1st to answer the question regarding the validity of the rapture while revealing God's true plan for His Church and I believe we have accomplished that mission. 2nd as a prelude to my next book regarding the nature and mission of the Kingdom of God. This book will remove all the mystery, speculation and misconceptions concerning what the Kingdom of God is, when it came, how it works and what mission it is to fulfill.

This book will make your heart beat passionately with true purpose and fulfillment as you discover, you are at the heart of God's plan concerning His Kingdom and its mandate. Your life does matter!

PARTNER WITH PASTOR PONCE LEON

Again, I want to personally thank you for investing in this book and invite you to Partner with Ponce Leon Ministries. It is my passion and mission in life to see the nations of this earth come to Jesus. A big part of seeing this come to pass is helping the Church to understand and fully believe that it is God's plan to fulfill the Great Commission. I want them to understand that not only is it possible, but that it will happen. I want the church to be gripped with the truth that the Gates of Hell set up on every nation, shall not prevail against the Church. For we are victorious, we will overcome and we will, through the Holy Spirit, kick down every gate of hell, in every nation, and they will be discipled, thus fulfilling the Great Commission.

If this message burns in your heart as it does mine. I invite you to partner with me to get this message out to believers in every nation. Go to PonceLeon.tv and click partner.

Thank you very much, and God bless you!

Pastor Ponce Leon

ABOUT THE AUTHOR

Ponce Leon pastors Victorious Faith Center in Apache, OK and leads Ponce Leon Ministries where he teaches the Finished Work of Jesus Christ with special emphasis on your Kingdom Purpose. His goal is to help enable the Body of Christ to grow into Christ's fullness to be empowered to live lives that impact destiny.

Learn more:

PonceLeon.tv

Facebook.com/PonceLeonMinistries

Youtube.com/PonceLeonMinistries

Instagram.com/PonceLeon.tv

96198629R00099

Made in the USA
Middletown, DE
29 October 2018